HOW TO GROW YOUR HOSPITALITY BUSINESS

A guide for owners and managers

Celia Hay

**H&H
PUBLISHING**

Christchurch New Zealand

CONTENTS

PREFACE Falling for Food..Page 7

CHAPTER ONE Home Grown Hospitality.....................................Page 9
New Zealand has been a late starter in the hospitality game but, since 1989, it
has impatiently adopted a café lifestyle. This chapter looks at the influences that
have created the change. It explains many of the French terms that are commonly
used but frequently misunderstood. From *la grande cuisine* to *nouvelle cuisine*,
from *brasserie* to *bistro*.

CHAPTER TWO So you want to be a Host ....Page 15
This is the business of celebration. Being a host comes naturally and most of
us wish to share our abundance and also enjoy making others feel welcome.
This chapter discusses the concept of *Host*, how to create a hospitality experience
and suggests ways to evaluate how you would fare in this role. The *Equation
of Satisfaction* is defined. It is simple to grasp but not so easy to implement.
This chapter also discusses the phenomenon of the *Hospitality Business Life Cycle*.

CHAPTER THREE That Great Idea: Finding a Market...........................Page 29
How do you start developing a great idea? What unique experience will you offer?
This chapter considers the vision for your product and what you are trying to
achieve. Looking at those businesses that have got it right offers inspiration to
the novice. Market segmentation provides new opportunities and conducting an
external analysis enables you to assess your customers, competitors, the market
and the business environment.

CHAPTER FOUR Setting Up – Knowing those Costs............................Page 53
What do you need to know to set up a hospitality business? During the planning
stage the excitement and anticipation is often tempered by the harsh reality of
costs and compliance. Some fundamental accounting principles are explained
along with key hospitality ratios that evaluate how a business is performing.
This chapter lists an overview of the legislation that affects a hospitality business.

CHAPTER FIVE The Menu as a Management Tool ....Page 69
Food and beverages are the products that we sell. Together they must provide
sufficient income to pay for all the business expenses, repay the debts and give
some return on the investment. This chapter discusses the theory of costing as
well as the economic concepts surrounding price sensitivity and the effect of
substitutes on the demand for your product.

CHAPTER SIX Constructing a Menu...Page 81
The menu is the key marketing tool for a café or restaurant. It projects the
personality of the place and communicates a message to the diners and
prospective diners. The menu must embody the vision and therefore be consistent
with the goals of the business. This chapter explains how to construct and cost
a menu and wine list as well as the principles of matching food and wine.

CHAPTER SEVEN Building a Team..Page 93
What is the role of an owner or manager? How do you build a motivated team that supports you and your vision? This chapter looks at what it takes to be an effective leader who can motivate and inspire a team. Trust, communication, commitment and accountability underscore the characteristics of a leader. The chapter also discusses negotiation techniques and how to run successful meetings.

CHAPTER EIGHT Employing the Right People...................................Page 103
The hospitality industry employs many people. This chapter discusses how to employ the right people and then train them to do a great job. It assesses the roles of the chef and manager and how to balance the different responsibilities of each job. It looks at how conflict can arise between the kitchen staff and the waiting staff. The recruitment process is explained along with interviewing techniques and how to write an advertisement.

CHAPTER NINE Achieving the Standard...Page 121
Achieving the standard is about serving safe food and having competent, well informed staff who understand the concept of quality. This chapter discusses operational issues such as greeting, seating and meeting the customers' expectations as well as the importance of building relationships with your customers. What does your body language tell the customers about how you feel today? What is quality? Safe food and the responsibilities of the hospitality business are also considered.

CHAPTER TEN Hospitality Marketing..Page 143
Marketing is the way to stay in business. Having the vision to build a brand will become the most important element in creating a competitive advantage for a hospitality business. The goal is to create an image and a presence in the marketplace. A simple action plan can be the most effective marketing strategy. This chapter also discusses the importance of public relations and how to write a press release.

CHAPTER ELEVEN So You Made It..Page 159
To stay ahead and maintain a competitive advantage you must innovate, refresh and reinvent your product. This chapter discusses strategies for renewal. You cannot do this if you are worn out, grumpy and do not enjoy going to work. Renewal is as important on a personal level as it is for a business. It is often at this stage that the manager leaves and the business is sold.

APPENDIX...Page 167
1. Costing exercise to try yourself.
2. Set up costs. A comprehensive list of the set-up costs for a hospitality business, from the number of ladles to the contents of the cleaning cupboard.
3. Bibliography

ACKNOWLEDGEMENTS

In writing this book I have discovered that I actually like to write. Fortunately my network includes a number of erudite souls who have taken time to read and comment on the text. I am grateful for their observations. David Burton, Ray McVinnie and Hugh Wall at Christchurch Polytechnic who have looked at the content of this book from their diverse hospitality experiences. Lisa Scholz from Saggio di Vino who has contributed an international perspective on service delivery and running a restaurant as well as Joanna McLeod who advised on other aspects of the book and Professor Don Beaven the *chief dispenser of enthusiasm* who evaluated the chapter on menus and wine lists.

To my editor Sue Zydenbos for her comments and direction, Donna Hoyle for the stylish book design and Anthony McKee for the photographs.

To my three boys who patiently put up with my projects.

To the dedicated team both past and present at Hay's and the School who have helped me realise my vision. In particular Liliane Huckle who only wanted to work for six months and is still with us five years later. To Evan Michelson and Gabrielle Lewis who have joined us more recently. To Lois Blackie and Victoria Herman who still hold the vision even though they no longer work at Hay's.

And to all the students of the New Zealand School of Food and Wine, without whom, this book would never exist.

Succeeding in any business, whether as a manager or owner, cannot be taken for granted. Business is dynamic. There is always something to attend to, some riddle to solve. The better you understand what it takes to be successful, the greater your chances of success.

This book looks at the cafés, restaurants and bars of New Zealand's hospitality industry. It provides a framework for would-be owners as well as aspiring managers and students of hospitality. The book draws on my experience of growing five different businesses and incorporates what I consider to be the foundations for success.

For those wanting to rush in and establish a business, this is a cautionary tale. The set-up can be the easy part. Staying in business and growing the business can provide the most challenge.

Falling for Food

Food. *It rules our lives.* In the past we ate for energy and to survive. Today we eat for a myriad of reasons. Food can be our reward. It can provide the pivotal part of a celebration. Food can be the celebration. Food is so central to our lives that we all have an opinion on what is good food and what is bad. This emotional attachment evokes numerous responses especially when dining out. We know what we like and when we are paying, we are quick to judge. Since the mid-1980s New Zealanders have fallen for food.

As a young woman I returned from three years overseas, full of food experiences. My travels had become a culinary voyage, each destination characterised by the eating experienced. Chillies, cumin and coriander in Mexico; a fresh mango traded for cheese and crackers at the foot of Half Dome in Yosemite National Park; globe artichokes with a piquant vinaigrette in Provence; a month in Tuscany with an Italian family; nine months in India. As I write I still remember the sensation and excitement of discovering new tastes. Back in Christchurch, blessed with some entrepreneurial zeal, I soon found myself in business. Initially in retail with a boutique card and stationery shop called Cartouche, but within eighteen months I had expanded to food.

My sister Gill had returned from abroad as well. She liked to cook and I was eager to establish a range of preserves, emulating the Crabtree and Evelyn concept, to sell at Cartouche and wholesale nationally. For several months we made the preserves at Cracroft House, the Girl Guide Centre, using their commercial kitchen. We then found a shop in Holmwood Road, Fendalton. The Preservatory Delicatessen was opened in December 1985. The Delicatessen took over and the jams were put on the back-burner while we concentrated on growing the business. I sold Cartouche soon after in 1987.

In those first years at the Preservatory even muffins were new. The supermarkets did not offer gourmet cheese and on a Friday we would sell five kilos of brie cut to order. We also did a roaring trade of French brie at $59 per kilo. The Preservatory made its own pâté plus lots of salads, quiche, pies and cakes. On a Saturday morning, we would have a queue out the door. In 1988, a second delicatessen, The Preservatory Kilmore, was opened on the corner of Victoria and Kilmore Streets. During the winter of 1990 we ran our first cooking demonstrations which became an annual feature. Gill and I dissolved our business partnership in 1993 and in 1994 I set up Hay's Café, now called Hay's, at 63 Victoria Street. The New Zealand School of Food and Wine was established on the floor above in 1995.

My history parallels the changes in hospitality in New Zealand. Like many young people who travelled overseas, I wanted to enjoy the food that I had experienced. I liked to experiment in the kitchen and attempt to recreate the flavours I had tasted. The Preservatory was a start, and as this business developed so too did my need to find out more; to understand the philosophy of the French masters and what it takes to run a successful hospitality business.

When I organised the first cooking school programme in 1990, I became the chief beneficiary of these classes. In that first year our guests included a selection of culinary luminaries including Catherine Bell, Annabel Langbein, Allyson Gofton and Lauraine Jacobs, to name just a few. Jo Seagar's exuberance as a food communicator was evident then. I learnt the most from Graham Brown of Scarborough Fare, whose dedication to creating wonderful food was truly inspirational. From Greg Heffernan, then at Huka Lodge, I learnt about a sophisticated style of cooking that at the time, was rare to find in New Zealand. Through the generosity of Kingsley Wood, area manager of Liquorland at that time, I was able to offer wine matches with the menus and in doing so I began my wine education.

CHAPTER ONE

HOME GROWN HOSPITALITY

Cafés first emerged in Paris in the late seventeenth century. They were *houses of coffee*, where people read the paper, played chess, debated politics and ate light meals. This phenomenon finally reached New Zealand in the 1980s. We had coffee shops and sandwich bars but aside from the rare exception, these were simple establishments with plain counter food and poor coffee. They could not offer alcohol as an alternative beverage. In this chapter the concept of café and restaurant is explored.

In the 1990s coffee bars became a central component of the American social scene, in part because they fulfilled the need for a non-threatening gathering spot, a "third place" outside of work and home...

Howard Schultz,
Pour your heart into it

HOSPITALITY CHANGES. In New Zealand, the catalyst that caused the café rush was a new Sale of Liquor Act, passed in 1989. This Act acknowledged that times had changed. Cheap international air fares and television had brought the world closer and with it, the desire of the consumer to imitate what was happening abroad. New Zealand was now part of the international trend toward a more sophisticated and accessible dining experience. Eating out was no longer the preserve of the wealthy. Prior to the new Act, it had been very difficult to gain a liquor licence. This was a legacy of the prohibition movement, whose other great contribution was gaining the vote for women in 1893. A number of referenda had been held in the first two decades of the early 20th century. The prohibition lobby would have won, had it not been for the votes of the servicemen in 1917. Older readers will recall a referendum on liquor licensing at each election until 1978. There were three choices: State Control, Continuance (status quo) or Prohibition. It was not until 1967, that the 50-year tradition of the *6 o'clock swill*, the closing the pubs at 6.00 pm, was changed to 10.00 pm.

New Zealand's first licensed restaurants appeared in the 1950s. They were formal dining rooms where alcohol was served with dinner. It was not possible to go for a casual glass of wine. Hours of trade were restricted and by the 1980s *bring your own* (BYO) restaurants were still far more common than licensed ones. Once the restaurants closed and the pubs shut, people just went home. There was nowhere to go. Eating brunch on a Saturday or Sunday, other than at a hotel, was a thing of the future. I still get international tourists at Hay's telling me they came to New Zealand in the 1970s and everything was shut. The only place to eat was either the hotel or the local fish and chip shop. These people are quick to add that they can not believe the improvement in the quality of food and wine now served in New Zealand!

The Sale of Liquor Act 1989 removed significant obstacles to obtaining liquor licences. Under the new legislation, if you were of good character and complied with local government and health requirements, you could secure a liquor licence. Overnight, existing BYO restaurants applied to sell liquor and waited the many months that this application took to process. Bars selling better quality food and coffee as well as the normal range of beers and spirits were established. Quality wine became available by the glass. No one was quite sure what to call these establishments and they often became known as *café-bars* or just *cafés*.

Against union opposition, Saturday trading had started in the early 1980s. The Employment Contracts Act 1991 provided another stimulant to weekend trade as employers were able to negotiate employment contracts without union input. With the abolition of penal rates, the cost of opening on a Saturday or Sunday dropped significantly. Suddenly hospitality businesses started to open seven days a week and some even secured a 24-hour liquor licence. Consumers quickly adopted the concept of 24-hour hospitality. This change in lifestyle has given New Zealand an aura of sophistication that was lacking when it was not possible to buy a drink past 11 pm or go out for a Sunday lunch and enjoy a glass of wine.

Food Tourism. Hospitality has become a major employer in New Zealand and the industry is intrinsically tied to tourism. When people travel, what they eat is crucial to their impression. The more people travel, the more discerning they become, particularly with regard to food. Tour operators rely on the hospitality industry to provide a quality eating experience. Market segments have emerged for food tourism. France has known this for generations, but the rest of the world is discovering that visitors will travel a great distance to indulge in the pleasures of the table.

THE FRENCH TRADITION. The French culinary tradition has developed over hundreds of years. In 1825, Brillat-Savarin, wrote in his legendary book *The Physiology of Taste* about the significance of gastronomy. *"Gastronomy is the reasoned comprehension of everything connected with the nourishment of man ... ... (it) supports us from the table to the grave ... lends new delights to love, strengthens the bonds of friendship, disarms hatred, facilitates the conduct of affairs, and offers us, during our brief span of life, the only pleasure which, having no aftermath of weariness, remains to refresh us after all the rest?"*[1]

Curnonsky (1872–1956) the famous French food writer described four distinct styles of French Cookery.[2]

1. *Haute cuisine*, also called *la grande cuisine*, was the food of royalty and the upper classes, cooked by the legendary French chefs in large hotels, estates and palaces. The food was complicated, time-consuming and involved many chefs in the preparation of intricate sauces and garnishes. It was culinary art.
2. *La cuisine bourgeoise* referred to the food of the middle classes cooked each day for the family.
3. *La cuisine régionale*[3] became a marriage of gastronomy and tourism focused on the fresh, local produce (*produits de terroir*) that was currently in season.
4. *La cuisine improvisée* was about making do with whatever was available!

The famous chefs were practitioners of *haute cuisine*. These chefs included La Varenne (1618–1678), Carême (1774–1833) and more recently Auguste Escoffier (1846–1935). La Varenne is remembered as the author of one of the first cook books to be published. Escoffier collaborated with hotelier César Ritz (1850–1918) to establish the Grand Hotel of Monte Carlo and the Savoy in London as well as other renowned hotels in Europe. The best hotels of Europe used French chefs and because of this a French culinary imperialism was established.[4] Escoffier also wrote a number of books and the most famous *Le Guide Culinare* (1903) is still in print today. His recipes are the foundation of modern French Cuisine. In *Le Guide Culinare* he collated many of the traditional recipes that had previously been passed down by word of mouth. Today these recipes are still regarded as classics and the basic recipes may not have changed for 200 years.

Escoffier's famous *"faites simple"*, keep it simple, is still resonated today by cooks around the world. Escoffier is also remembered for establishing the *partie* system which is still in use in commercial kitchens. This organises the kitchen staff by breaking down the functions into sections, each headed by a *chef de partie*.

Different styles of eating establishments grew out of differing demands. At the top of the scale were the *restaurants* of *haute cuisine*. Following this were *brasseries* and *bistros*, with the *café* being the simplest form of a hospitality business. The term *restaurant*, from the verb to restore (*restaurer*), became popular following the French Revolution in 1789. Many excellent chefs found their patrons had suffered under the guillotine. They now set up in business themselves.[4] Today the great restaurants of France and other parts of Europe are easily identified by the annual award of Michelin Stars. The Michelin Red Guide was first published in 1900 and since 1926 has awarded stars to rank the restaurant. At a *one star* the cuisine would be described as *"very good cooking"*, at a *two star* it would be described as *"excellent cooking"*. The ultimate three stars is an award for *"exceptional cuisine, worth a special journey, superb wine, faultless service, elegant surroundings. One will pay accordingly!"*[5] By 2000, there were still only 22 three-star restaurants in France.

The *brasserie* was originally a German brewery with wooden benches and tables. These became popular in France after 1870. Today it is commonly used to describe a large establishment where beer, wine and coffee is served with a limited all-day menu. A *bistro* is a small, modest restaurant. The term appeared in the French language in 1884.[6] Its origin is thought to be Russian for "quick". These are usually family restaurants and offer a small menu often featuring regional dishes. Some may serve a set menu or *table d'hôte* with a *prix fixe* (fixed price) at a communal table, while others offer a *plat du jour* (daily specials). The *à la carte* menu is also widely used.

A café was originally called a *maison de café* and the first records date from 1672.[7] Coffee was originally thought to be a cure for alcoholism! Later cafés began selling beer, wine and offering small meals. During the 19th century, the Parisian cafés became more fashionable and sophisticated. The décor became more elaborate and the prices more expensive. In the early 20th century, the less formal corner café was established. This was open from breakfast until late at night, serving both coffee and wine as well as light meals. The *cafeteria* is a 20th century concept that came into use in the 1950s. This is a self-service restaurant with prepared counter food.

Haute cuisine has barely been experienced in New Zealand, except perhaps for the Governor General's table or the wealthy élite who could afford to employ a classically trained chef. Our food has always been much simpler and of a regional character. Food historian Tony Simpson[8] talks of the importance of meat to the settlers. To them meat was a symbol of economic success. They had been deprived of meat in their European homes and, once it became affordable and accessible, meat would be consumed three times a day. Fish, an ingredient plentiful in New Zealand, was largely ignored by the European settlers.

NOUVELLE CUISINE. In 1972, a phenomenon called *nouvelle cuisine* emerged in France. It was a call to simplify the *haute cuisine* and return to the authentic flavours of the fresh ingredients. If the dish was described as rabbit, it should taste like rabbit. Conscious about fat, a new generation of *chef-patrons*, chefs who now owned their own restaurants, had emerged during the 1960s. These chefs took up the challenge to create a more healthy style of cuisine, reducing the amount of fat and simplifying the cooking methods to retain some nutritional value. For example, the mounting with butter (*monter au beurre*) to give the sauce a rich sheen, and flour liaisons (using flour and butter as thickener), were replaced with sauces based on reduction.

The food processor was a new innovative tool in the kitchen and enabled chefs to experiment in novel ways. Any food could be chopped or puréed in a matter of seconds. Previously this had been a time-consuming task. Chefs sought to create edible works of art. To do this the chef now plated the food in the kitchen to achieve the level of presentation required rather than let the waiting staff portion it at the table. At its height of popularity, *nouvelle cuisine* was colourful baby food, which lacked texture, protein and starch. Consumers rebelled and demanded a meal of more substance that would leave them replete.

During the 1980s, multicultural California led the way in combining Asian ingredients with French tradition. Add to this the rediscovery of Italian food, and a new international style of cuisine had emerged. Television chef, Ken Hom, described this new cuisine in a 1987 *Australian Gourmet* magazine. *"A cooking style that emphasises the blending of foods, spices, flavourings and techniques formerly isolated from each other within Asian and European kitchens ... When East meets West, we see not a hodge podge but a thoughtful, graceful and delectable blending of appropriate elements."*

For a short while this style was referred to as *East-West* or *Californian* cuisine. It was adopted by the innovative, young Australian chefs who started to refer to the style as *Fusion* or *Pacific Rim* cuisine. Chefs in New Zealand quickly embraced the concept. While there is still no consensus on what the name to describe this style should be, there is agreement on the fact that ingredients should be fresh, local if possible, and not overwhelmed by a confusion of different flavours. Pacific Rim cuisine remains essentially European in technique and it is only by the addition of Asian flavours that it is differentiated.

Educating the palates of New Zealanders has been interesting to watch. New Zealanders are innovators in some regards particularly in the adoption of a coffee culture. Offered a braised cock's comb or poached lamb brains, however, we would run a mile. We are still a country of conservative diners.

1. Brillat-Savarin. *The Physiology of Taste,* 1970.
2. David, E. *French Provincial Cooking,* 1960.
3. Reardon, J. *Celebrating the Pleasures of the Table,* 1994.
4. *Food, A Culinary History,* 1999.
5. Millon, M. T*he Food Lover's Companion to France,* 1996.
6. *Larousse Gastronomique,* 1990.
7. *Food, A Culinary History,* 1999.
8. Simpson, T. *A Distant Feast,* 1999.

CHAPTER TWO

SO YOU WANT TO BE A HOST?

People go into business for a variety of reasons. Some want to provide employment for themselves, while others are motivated by the challenge of being their own boss. The hospitality industry is an attractive investment as it has comparatively low start-up costs. It is also enticing because eating and drinking is something that we do every day and therefore it makes everyone an expert! In this chapter the concept of *Host* is examined along with how to create a hospitality experience. The life cycle of a hospitality business is also discussed.

I want people to share the excitement of good things, beautiful foodstuffs, little lettuces from our garden, herbs in bloom, a gnarly local pippin from somebody's old tree – and if I can see that people are receptive, then something wonderful happens: time stops – you're a child again, but still an adult and not just a satisfied, pleasure seeking hedonist, but a participant in something shared: And you know, it may not matter whether or not the souffle turned out perfectly.

Alice Waters of Chez Panisse
in **Celebrating the Pleasures of the Table**

WHAT MAKES A GOOD HOST. People are attracted to hospitality because of the concept of *Host*. Being a host fulfils something innately human in all of us.

"I am a good host, I like to entertain ... "

"I take pleasure in cooking for others ... "

"I enjoy the whole experience, the cooking, the conviviality, the shared table ... "

Being a good host is the willingness to share our abundance. Understanding this urge within yourself can be a great motivational force. For many in this industry this is the *raison d'être*. It is a simple thing to get pleasure from making other people happy and when people are genuinely appreciative of your efforts, it is enormously satisfying. It spurs you on to do it again and again. Night after night. You can feel a sense of satisfaction when your diners complement you on your efforts.

> **What makes a good host?**
> - The genuine desire to make someone feel welcome, comfortable and to share your table with them.
> - A generous and giving nature.
> - Being good company.
> - An understanding of taste.
> - The ability to efficiently meet and anticipate the customer's needs.

In order to be a good host, you must also understand good food and in particular, taste. A host must be a gourmand. Brillat-Savarin defines gourmandism as an *"act of judgement, by which we give preference to things which are agreeable to our taste over those which are not"*.[1] Cooking is very creative and, like being a host, it fulfils a human urge to create. It can, therefore, be very gratifying to discover a diner's delight in what you love to do. There is another aspect to this industry that keeps participants young: adrenalin. *Ready, steady, GO!* When the restaurant is full, the kitchen is bustling and the customers are happy, it is exciting and very stimulating. With the chef's heart racing as each new order is called, it is *GO GO GO …* cook and perform. And this can happen every night. Middle-aged adventurers seek to relive their youth by climbing mountains and bungy jumping, however the chef gets to feel the adrenalin rush every night!

The business of celebration. As a manager or owner, it is important for you to understand your own motivations and what attracts you to the industry. It is easy for people to become involved in a hospitality businesses without full comprehension of what is involved. This is the business of celebration which means that you must work when everyone else wishes to celebrate: *Friday nights, Saturday nights, Sundays, Christmas Day, New Year's Eve, Mother's Day.* The *"I like to entertain"* group soon discover that a hospitality business is not just drinking with your customers or having friends around to dine on a feast created by your chef. Entertaining at home and the reality of running a hospitality business are two completely different things.

A little learning is a dangerous thing. Successful hospitality businesses specialise in making their hard work seem effortless. This is an illusion that the uninitiated fall for. Yes, it looks easy to walk around and efficiently take orders during a busy dinner service. It appears that way because the systems are in place. The waiting staff are trained and understand their role. The chef is experienced and can handle any situation. The team works together to create a faultless dining experience. This scenario is true for all hospitality businesses whether it is a casual café or an overcrowded bar.

IS THIS YOU?

- I need a job.

- I am sick of working for others. I want financial independence and to enjoy the profits of my hard work.

- I've got my nest egg and now I want to invest in something I enjoy myself.

- I like the idea of being a host and sharing my place with you.

- It's easy to cook, I like it and it's fun. My friends say that I am a great cook. I want to develop this skill.

- Why is restaurant food so bad? I can cook better than this at home!

- I like to cook. It fulfils a creative urge within me. I would like to own my own place so that I can pursue this.

- I like the buzz, the busyness, the adrenalin of the rush.

- Remember the TV show *Cheers*? I like the idea of having a place where my friends can meet and we can chat and drink ... *"Where everybody knows your name ... "*

- It's so social. I love meeting people and I am a people person. I'm good with people.

- The hours suit me while I study. All my friends drink there so why shouldn't I get paid to have a good time.

Many newcomers underestimate how much this industry revolves around cleaning. After a busy lunch or dinner service there is always the cleaning to be done. Cleaning the café, clearing the dishes, washing the dishes, polishing the cutlery and glasses, wiping the tables and re-setting the tables. In the kitchen there is a constant flow of dirty dishes, pots and pans, messy benches, filthy hobs and greasy grills. On top of this list are other chores. Who will clean the toilets? Who will clean the floors? Who will weed the garden? For the consumer, it is easy to judge how much a business values cleanliness; the toilets are often the most telling example. The state of the kitchen staff uniforms is also an indication.

HOSPITALITY IS ABOUT EXPERIENCE. The environment welcomes the diner. The smile of the person behind the counter, the look of the décor, the ambience, the music, all add to the experience. The happy-hum of a busy business run by competent and energetic people are characteristics of a successful hospitality business. The quality of the food served reinforces the experience. Food at its most basic level is about satisfying the senses, such as the look (*colour, presentation*), smell (*what does it remind you of?*) and above all the taste. You hear other customers' complimentary comments; you see the food go by.

> *"Hmmmm, that looks nice"*
> *"I wonder what they are eating over there?"*

After the first mouthful, you just want to eat more. The flavours; the feel of the food in the mouth push you to continue eating and to enjoy the sensory experience.

American business writer Tom Peters, talks of the *"Pursuit of WOW!"*[2] What he means is *"stepping out and standing out from the growing crowd of look-alikes"*. He talks of enlivening the senses and fulfilling unexpressed wishes. Being average has never had much appeal. He writes *"to … look … feel … to taste … touch … sound … smell … texture … colour … typeface (on logos, letterheads, etc.) And it adds up to … ? E-X-P-E-R-I-E-N-C-E!"*[3] …

A QUALITY EXPERIENCE. Quality is essential for a good hospitality experience, not just in food but also in service. There is food and then there is **excellent** food. In producing excellent food there are some basic assumptions that underlie what it takes to make it good.

Characteristics of quality/excellent food.[4] The list below discusses issues that are important to ensure quality food.
- **Produce.** This should be fresh, seasonal and of good quality.
- **Safety.** Food must be safe. Diners do not expect to suffer from a bout of food poisoning!
- **Look.** Food should be visually exciting, making use of interesting combinations of ingredients for colour and texture.
- **Taste.** Food is flavoursome. The taste should make a diner want to eat another mouthful.
- **Finished.** Food is finished when it leaves the kitchen. A diner should not have to season a meal.
- **Consistent.** The quality of the meal must be consistent. If a diner returns next week and orders the same meal, it should be of a very similar standard.

Characteristics of quality service. Like food, there are some fundamental assumptions that determine whether or not you are receiving quality service. The list below discusses issues that are important to ensure quality service.

- **Tangibles.** The appearance of physical facilities, décor, ambience and how the staff look.
- **Reliability.** The ability to perform and deliver what the business has said that it is going to do.
- **Responsiveness.** To actively listen to customer requests and respond efficiently, e.g. special dietary requirements.
- **Competence.** Staff that display skill and knowledge.
- **Empathy.** Individual attention by staff who care about what the diner thinks.

Signals of high quality. Beyond the classifications set out above, are a series of customer perceptions that influence whether or not a product is perceived as being of good quality. These perceptions are often linked to the image of the brand. *"It's from Harrod's so it must be of good quality."* The quality of the experience of eating chocolates from Fortnum and Mason will only be enhanced if the consumer identifies with the brand. For someone who has never heard of Fortnum and Mason, the specialness and therefore the perception of quality, will be lost.

Perceptions of high quality – some popular examples:
- Salmon. The pinker the salmon the better the flavour.
- Tomato juice. The thicker the juice the higher the quality.
- Orange juice. Fresh is better than refrigerated, which is superior to bottled.
- Wine. The higher the price the better the quality.
- Flowers. Fresh flowers are superior to dried.
- Hand towels. Presentation of warmed hand towels to diners displays higher quality than paper towels.
- Tablecloths. Starched white linen tablecloths are superior to no tablecloths.

Denotes lower quality
- Formica tables
- Plastic wine corks
- Cask wine
- Instant coffee
- Paper napkins
- Substitute cream

THE EXPERIENCE. A hospitality business must be built around understanding the experience that you wish to create. Some of the features that you would expect a café, bar or restaurant to have are described below.

The Café Experience ... *what makes it special?*
- The unique personality of the owner.
- The chef cooks great food.
- There is a particular brand of coffee that may be unavailable elsewhere.
- The décor fits with the style of the business.
- The location gives profile or is convenient.
- The staff are well organised and have a helpful attitude.
- The food selection consists of gutsy flavours, some counter food that is ready to eat immediately and interesting daily specials.
- The food and beverages are moderately priced.
- The wine list is small but well chosen with a good selection of wines by the glass at a variety of prices.
- The ambience is noisy, busy and fun. There is music with character.
- The service and food delivery are fast.

The Café-Bar Experience ... *what makes it special?*
- The unique personality of the owner.
- Often a café-bar is really just a bar.
- More alcohol is drunk than coffee, although coffee is for sale.
- Food is not a priority although it should be. Simple meals are served, such as antipasto platters, bar snacks, etc.
- The beer, wine and spirit selection is extensive.
- There is a variety of prices to meet a variety of customer needs.
- The décor fits with the style of the business.
- The location gives profile or convenience.
- The staff are well organised with a helpful attitude.

The Restaurant Experience ... *who is the hero?*
- The food sets the standard.
- The chef is the hero?
- The owner is the hero?
- The staff must be competent and professional.
- The décor and lighting must create atmosphere and ambience.
- The chairs should be comfortable so that diners will be happy to sit for several hours.
- The location is important. A restaurant can become a destination.
- The level of the background music enables diners to communicate.
- A good wine list is offered with reasonable choice at a variety of prices.

HOW LONG? If a small business is to become a bigger business, then it does take time and resources. Much comes down to the vision of the individual. Unfortunately many people go into a hospitality business with an unrealistic time frame and imagine that they will be able to sell within two or three years. This strategy is flawed. It is the exception where someone can sell their business in a short time and make a high profit. Unfortunately, as with real estate, it is often the exception that it thought to be the rule and erroneously drives demand.

If you know the industry well and are prepared to work hard then of course you can sell your business in two or three years. This strategy, however, can only be for people with experience who know how to grow a business and have a well functioning team. They understand their cost structure, what it takes to break even and the prices that they need to charge. Experienced people know how to establish a business. They work hard, are prepared to leave money in the business and do not have expectations of a high salary during the start up phase. They can show a good set of accounts, sell the business, take the capital gain and move on.

The problem often for this group is what to do next? The *host* aspect of this industry makes this business a way of life. If you are a natural host, then this is not going to disappear as soon as the business is sold. In fact, with a holiday and time to evaluate the options, many people realise that all they want to do is to become a host again. This means establishing another business. It also means starting from the beginning. In hindsight, they realise that they would have been better to manage the business to a point where it was possible to delegate to someone else. This would enable them to take a holiday and renew themselves and their enthusiasm.

A short term strategy can also mean that you do not see the opportunities that may present themselves if you plan on being around longer. It may mean that you invest in inferior equipment: a domestic stove rather than a commercial one; formica benches over stainless steel. It may mean that you do not spend so much energy in developing a competent and loyal team. For the business to grow, a long term strategy is needed. I would say that three years is the minimum length of time. By five years you have become established and have a loyal clientèle.

BUSINESS LIFE CYCLE. Hospitality businesses, like other businesses, have a life cycle. The diagram below appears in *The Small Business Book* by Bob Hamilton and John English.[5] They have taken the marketing concept of a Product Life Cycle and extended it to a Small Business Life Cycle. In marketing terms, a product life cycle shows the sales of a product as it moves through four stages:

Product Life Cycle: introduction → growth → maturity → decline

**Small Business
Life Cycle:**   start-up   → take-off → harvest → renewal

SMALL BUSINESS LIFE CYCLE

Phase	Start-up	Take-off	Harvest	Renewal
Goal	Survival	Sales	Profits	Revival
Role	Initiator Innovator Organiser	Developer Implementer Delegator	Administrator Manager Leader	Successor Reorganiser Revitaliser
Typical crises	Confidence Cash flow	Cash flow Delegation	Leadership Complacency	Inertia Succession

Hamilton, R. and English, J. *The Small Business Book*, 3rd ed, 1997.

For companies with multiple products, it is important to always have new products in the development phase to replace those reaching decline. It is easy to see the dynamics of a product life cycle working within a menu as new dishes sell well at first and then over time become less attractive. It is at this point that they need to be replaced.

The hospitality industry has essentially two products, food and beverage, which are linked by the service provided. Any new products are still in effect reinventions of the original products. This makes an equation which is easy to calculate.

Equation of satisfaction
Good product   +   Good service   =   Customer satisfaction
Good product   +   Bad service   =   Customer dissatisfaction
Bad product   +   Good service   =   Customer dissatisfaction

Start-up. The start-up phase for many businesses is both exciting and terrifying. It is full of opportunity, hope and fear. Many businesses fail at this stage. They run out of cash and agonise over their direction and strategy. The main goal for the business is to survive. Cash is the lifeblood of the business. To survive, it must have cash. To have cash the business must innovate to convince people to buy the product. Unfortunately the fight to survive often results in poor or impulsive decisions, made because the owner is desperate rather than for their strategic benefit. The owner can become emotionally exhausted and focused on keeping the business going rather than seeing opportunities for growth. It was at this point that, strapped for cash to expand the Body Shop, Anita Roddick borrowed £4000 from a friendly garage owner and gave him 50% of the company.[6] She regretted the decision in the years that followed.

Take-off. In this stage, sales are going up and a competitive advantage is being built. The business requires more cash as investment is made in other equipment and staff. There are still cash flow problems but, given time, that elusive profit will be achieved. The manager has learnt to be innovative and has the confidence to delegate.

Harvest Phase. You have made it! Profit has been achieved and will be used to repay debt. The manager now focuses on costs and how to achieve further efficiencies. The rapid growth in sales may have slowed although the competitive advantage is now well established. Day to day procedures are in place but the manager is increasingly removed from these. The manager has learnt what it takes to be a good leader and how to foster commitment from the staff and customers. It is often at this stage that the manager starts to look elsewhere for new challenges. As a manager you may look for a new job. A holiday or sabbatical can be a positive solution. The owner can take time out, refocus and devise future strategies for growth. Failure to look ahead can undermine the business.

Renewal. In the renewal phase the owner or manager has often lost interest. Complacency can result in the business losing its competitive advantage. The owner or manager may resist the need to change or may have difficulty deciding how to progress. Unless there is new leadership with a new vision and strategy, the business will fail.

HOSPITALITY BUSINESS LIFE CYCLE. While hospitality businesses experience both the product life cycle and the small business life cycle, many also experience a variant of this which I have called the *Hospitality Business Life Cycle*. In a hospitality business the first six months can destroy a business.

HOSPITALITY BUSINESS LIFE CYCLE

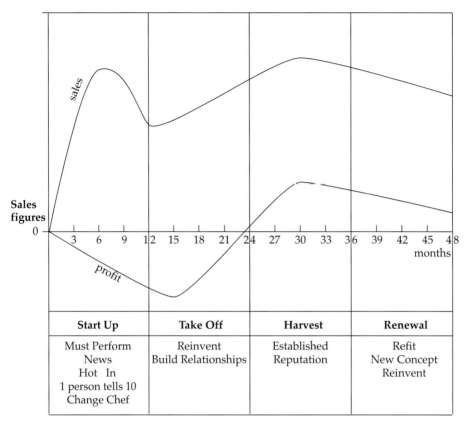

Start Up	Take Off	Harvest	Renewal
Must Perform News Hot In 1 person tells 10 Change Chef	Reinvent Build Relationships	Established Reputation	Refit New Concept Reinvent

Since the business has only two products and a service, it is critical that these products get through to the take-off phase of the life cycle. Most hospitality businesses will only reach the harvest phase of their life cycle by their fifth anniversary. The period from five to ten years can be very profitable. Usually during this period the business will need to develop strategies for renewal.

Characteristics of a new hospitality business. Overnight it becomes the place to eat. It's in the news, hot, trendy and fashionable. To ensure continued patronage the business must perform. It must deliver the equation of satisfaction. A good review in a local newspaper helps fuel demand. Each customer equates to a restaurant reviewer as the word of mouth process begins. They will recommend or criticise their experience. Often at this point you hear people say, *"I went to that new bar … last night, boy, was the service terrible. I had to wait 45 minutes for my meal and then the meal was mediocre"*.

Service consultants are always quick to say that one person tells ten people when they have had a bad experience. In the hospitality industry, if a place is new, there is a lot of talk and gossip. Lauraine Jacobs, a writer and restaurant reviewer for *Cuisine* magazine, argues that service is more important than the food *"if the service is good, people will keeping going back even if the food is not great"*. Getting the service right from day one with new staff and untested procedures is a difficult task. Experienced operators will always open quietly to ensure that the systems are in place before they start promotion. With prominent locations however, it is hard to control the flow of customers when you first open the doors. People have heard the talk and seen the building being fitted out. Their curiosity is aroused. This stage can be the most damaging for the business. People will come once and if they are not satisfied they will be slow to return. And they will tell all their friends of their dreadful experience. This is the most devastating scenario for a new business. It can take years to get those customers back through the doors again.

In the following chart, we can see that a hospitality business, may go through one iteration of the business life cycle in the first twelve months. The initial six months are characterised by people trying the business out. Sales can be high but profits are not. Problems with costing the menu and achieving the right balance of food and beverage costs undermine the financial performance. Inexperienced staff put customers off. By six months the business has become old news. Unless the public hear good comments about the business, the interest in dining there wanes. Within the first twelve months the business may need to reinvent its products and work to regain those customers. This is achievable with a commitment to good food and service and some money to advertise. Over the next two years, sales should increase and with this, profitability.

Restaurants, bars and cafés who fail to recognise this cycle in the first twelve months will continue to struggle until they come up with ways of reinventing themselves. Necessity breeds innovation. The less money you have, the sooner you realise that you need to innovate to survive. A disenchanted public can be frustratingly indifferent to your need for their business.

Geoffrey Moore, the American marketing consultant[6], talks about a *Technology Adoption Cycle* and the process that it takes for people to adopt a product. At any time, he argues, only a small proportion will be the innovators but they are also the first people to move on. The goal is to get your product adopted. I have taken this concept and applied it to the hospitality industry.

Innovators

These are the first people through the door. They are enthusiasts and interested to try the product. If the experience is good they will support you. Either way, they will tell all their friends. They will also be the first group to move on to the next **new** place in town.

Early adopters

These are the people you could expect to see early in the product's lifecycle in the first three – six months.

Early majority

These people you could expect to see within twelve months when the business becomes more established and word-of-mouth starts to work.

Late majority

These are the people whom you may see between years one and three.

Laggards

These people ask you how long the business has been open when the business has just passed its fifth anniversary!

It is possible to pick up regular customers from each of those categories. Once the product has been satisfactorily evaluated it will be adopted.

For all hospitality businesses, time is the greatest asset. If the product is good and you have sufficient cash to get through the start-up phase, you will survive and prosper.

SELF EVALUATION

Go through the checklist and assess yourself

• What skills/hobbies do you have?
  What do you like to do with your spare time?

• What skills do others believe you have?

• What skills and experience will you bring to the business?

- Do you have the interpersonal skills that will enable you to build a team which understands the concept of host and supports your vision?

- Can you remain calm in the face of disgruntled customers?

- Can you accept that you may not be able to pay yourself much while your business gets established?

- Do you have the energy, commitment and patience to make this work?

- Will your family support you during this uncertain period?

The list below is a check list to work through when you start thinking about your business proposal. A bank would request similar information.

GUIDELINES ON HOW TO CONSTRUCT A BUSINESS PLAN

1.0 Introduction: Your vision and goals
This section includes a detailed description of your business proposal including the products and services.
- Describe ownership of the business and its legal structure.
- List the skills you will bring to the business.
- Conduct a competitor analysis where you discuss the competitive advantage that you will offer.

2.0 Marketing of the business
- Who will be your customers?
- Evaluate the demand for your products/service
- What will you charge for your product/service?
- How will the product be distributed?
- How will you advertise?

3.0 Finance
- How will you finance the business?
- List sources of equity capital.
- Prepare monthly budgets for the first two years.
- Provide a monthly cash-flow for first two years.
- Project annual balance sheets and profit and loss statements.
- Determine your breakeven point.

- Explain your personal balance sheet and how you will pay yourself.
- Who will be responsible for accounting?
- Discuss any agreements to lease property or plant.
- Discuss mortgages and personal guarantees that may be made.
- Consider *"what if"* to address negative situations.

4.0 Management and operations
- Discuss the organisational structure of the business.
- Identify the roles that the owners and key employees will play.
- Discuss the skills and experience that each brings to the business.
- How will the business be managed on a daily basis?

1. Brillat-Savarin. *The Physiology of Taste*, 1970.
2. Peters, T. *The Pursuit of WOW!* 1994.
3. Peters, T. *The Circle of Innovation*, 1997.
4. These characteristics have been developed around Aaker's Quality Dimensions in *Strategic Market Management*, 1995.
5. Hamilton, R. and English, J. *The Small Business Book*, 1997.
6. "Ian McGlinn's £4000 investment in The Body Shop was the best decision he ever made. When the company listed in 1984, his stake was worth £4 million, it is now worth in excess of £140 million pounds." Roddick, A. *Body and Soul*, 1991.
7. Moore, G. *Crossing the Chasm*, 1991.

CHAPTER THREE

THAT GREAT IDEA:
FINDING A MARKET

How do you start developing a great idea? What unique experience will you offer? This chapter considers the vision for your product and what you are trying to achieve. For a hospitality business, the experience that a customer encounters is of equal importance to the food eaten and the beverage imbibed. This chapter also looks at understanding how the marketplace will impact on your great idea.

In a sense the food industry today has realised an ancient dream. Democratic as well as oblivious of regional differences, it has made it possible for everyone to eat whatever they like whenever they like, albeit at a price.

Food: A Culinary History

Coming up with a great idea is easy for some people and extremely difficult for others. When an idea has been identified it is often referred to as a *window of opportunity*, and this combines the idea with the means to exploit it. Fortunately for the hospitality industry, most ideas are based around the two products of good food and good service. Unfortunately, those two products often become commodities that are not valued. The customer's perception of value varies from one person to the next. For the hospitality industry this perception often has more to do with the experience than anything else. For the diner, the experience may consist of feeling welcome and appreciated. It can consist of paying amazing attention to detail as the waiting staff anticipate the customer's every need. The experience can also relate to the décor or ambience.

VISION AND GOALS. A vision is a picture, a concept or an idea for a business. A vision provides a destination and is often encapsulated in a mission statement. This is usually one sentence that summarises what the organisation wishes to accomplish. Once the vision is determined, the goals by which you achieve the vision should be obvious. The goals provide a map which enables the destination to be reached. They can be both short term and long term; complicated or simple. The more complex a goal, the more human and financial resources are required. Two or three well chosen goals are far more achievable than ten goals.

Stephen Covey in his best seller, *The 7 Habits of Highly Effective People*,[1] tells his readers to *"Begin with the end in mind"*. To do this you must think through precisely what it is that you wish to do. Covey goes on to say that all things are created twice. First there is a mental creation where you dream and fantasise, plan and visualise. This can be very exciting and stimulating. Ideas come to you in the middle of the night. You may feel disturbed by the potential, invigorated by the opportunity and inspired by the possibilities.

The second creation is when you actually do it and physically build what you have planned in your mind. The second creation is never identical to the first, but the better you plan the more prepared you are.

The vision for the business and the objectives of the goals must be clear to all people who work in the organisation. If those people do not know or identify with the goals, it is impossible for them to work to attain them. Once the goals are clear, a strategy for achieving them is devised.

Some business consultants talk of *critical success factors* which are elements that will contribute most significantly to the success of the organisation. For a hospitality business these could be:

- *Ensuring the food is of a consistently high quality.*
- *Ensuring that the staff are informed and knowledgeable.*
- *Ensuring a quality experience for the diner.*

Defining the critical success factors for your organisation can provide you with a set of goals.

Strategy. A strategy is a commitment to undertake one set of actions rather than another.[2] The strategy focuses on resources that will be needed and an action plan to prioritise your energy. With a time frame to follow, it is easier to work through the process methodically. Patience and tenacity are required. There must be a willingness to stick to the strategy in the face of competition and adversity. Once you have achieved a goal it is important to recognise it and celebrate the accomplishment. With attainment, it is always salutary to evaluate what has happened with a sense of detachment. Was it good or bad? How could it have been done better?

HOW TO FIND A GREAT IDEA. Innovation in hospitality is a matter of degree. Often the idea is an old one in a new guise. In France, there are restaurants and cafés that have existed for 100 years just offering the same well-tried formula. The market for traditional custard squares, pies, filled rolls and sandwiches is well-established and this will still be the case in another twenty years. There will always be the opportunity to make the best sandwich or develop a reputation for the perfect pie that people seek out from all over the city.

Innovation may focus on a *look* or design element created by an architect or interior designer. In the early 1990s the Metropole in Parnell and Brasserie Flipp in Wellington were leaders in the *smart-casual* dining experience. These businesses had modern interiors, served creative and interesting food without the formality of a fine dining restaurant. Themes, such as the Southwest American look of Coyotes, a Christchurch café-bar, have captured people's imagination. There has been the stainless steel, mirrored walls and polished floor look, as well as the Mediterranean-style make-over. Starbucks, an American franchise, have introduced the concept of the *third place*[3]. This is a place that that feels like home with a décor that resembles someone's comfortable lounge.

The style of food also becomes a source of innovation. Strawberry Fare in Christchurch and Wellington introduced diners to a specialist dessert restaurant. Their market is predominantly female and they are often busiest at 10 o'clock at night when the after-theatre people arrive. Asian cuisines such as Indian, Thai or Malaysian food attract diners who frequently seek to relive their holiday experience. They offer inexpensive flavoursome food. Pedro's, a Christchurch restaurant established in 1980, specialises in seafood cooked in a Spanish and Basque style. The menu still includes dishes that appeared in those early days and this remains one of the most successful Christchurch restaurants. People go there for Pedro's distinctive style of cuisine.

Signature Dishes. The chef or restaurant can become known for a particular style of cooking and develop signature dishes that establish a reputation. However, this may then haunt them when the dish is removed from their menu. At Hay's we started specialising in lamb with a lamb burger which, in 1995, was an innovative idea. The idea was first suggested by the former Prime Minister, Mike Moore, as a means for more effective marketing of New Zealand Lamb.

Our burger had savoury minced lamb with garlic, fresh herbs and a dash of soy, a chunky tomato salsa, lettuce, avocado and sour cream. It was sandwiched between an olive bread bun. By 1998, as our style of food had become more sophisticated, I wanted to drop the lamb burger completely. It did not fit with the vision that I had for the business. My staff were reluctant to cut this signature dish and we debated the issue over many months. Then accidentally, when I was relieving while our chef, Liliane Huckle was on holiday, I inadvertently left the lamb burger off a reprint of the menu. It was gone. People still ask for it. Mavis Airey, the Food Editor at *The Press*, was incredulous that I should want to take it off. When Jo Seagar, exhausted after a day's book signing, requested a lamb burger, we made one to order!

There were two reasons why I took the lamb burger off the menu. The first reason was because it was café food and this was no longer the style of food that we wanted to present. As we had become more professional in our service delivery, we had ceased to be a café and had become a restaurant. In 1999 we even changed our name from Hay's Café to just Hay's. Like the lamb burger, however, the café name still sticks! The other reason for changing was that for a long time the lamb burger had been priced on the menu at $12.50. The lamb burger was a substitute for our more expensive dishes and therefore forced the average unit sales down. Why would some one pay $24 when they could enjoy a delicious lamb burger at $12.50?

New Twists. Bread is a staple of our diet. The arrival of Italian artisan breads in New Zealand is an example of an idea whose time had come. If Pandoro, the very successful Auckland bakery, had set up in the 1960s selling its products, the chances are the bakery would not have survived. This is because the experience of New Zealanders did not include an appreciation of the glory of Italian breads. Pandoro would have had to educate the public and create a demand. The fresh pasta business was slow to establish in the 1980s but by 1999 the home dinner replacement market had ensured that there was enough demand for a number of firms to compete with a range of excellent fresh pasta products.

The espresso coffee cart is a recent phenomenon. At fairs and busy town squares, people queue to have a fresh cup of good coffee. The overheads are low, depending mainly on the cost of the coffee machine. When trade drops off, you pack up and go home. This is a simple example of taking the product to the market. Similar food carts are also an easy way to get into business. Their major weakness is the poor personal hygiene standards of the operators which often puts customers off.

The growth of the wine industry in New Zealand has also provided opportunities for dining. In Marlborough both Jane Hunter and Allan Scott have demonstrated that it is possible to operate restaurants in tandem with wine sales. It gives patrons a chance to relax and taste the wines with appropriate food. A good food experience at a winery will engender positive thoughts when the patron recognises your wine label at the supermarket.

The accommodation sector has also discovered the importance of food in creating a competitive advantage. The George Hotel in Christchurch has established a fine reputation for its cuisine by employing a series of talented chefs over many years. The standard of the food adds to its competitive advantage. While the big hotels have always known this, small lodges and bed and breakfast businesses have now realised that food is part of their product mix. Inspired by the example of Huka Lodge, an accommodation experience of an international standard, many imitators have attempted to achieve the delicate balance of excellent accommodation, ambience, wine and food. The Wilderness Lodge, which was established first in Westland with a second lodge at Arthur's Pass, has successfully combined food accommodation and eco-tourism; the wilderness experience.

Location. The great idea may be the fact that you are the first person in the area to offer this service. Brigitte's, the Merivale café in Christchurch, was for years one of the few places to offer good espresso. Its location has always been an element of its success. An easily visible location on a busy street will help you convey your good idea to prospective customers. Location can also be about creating a destination where people come to you because they want what you have to offer. Stronechrubie, a restaurant with accommodation chalets located at Mt Somers near the Canterbury ski fields, has successfully achieved this.

Synergies. For many businesses their competitive advantage lies in the synergies that exist. Synergy can be defined as the whole being greater than the individual parts, for example 2+2=5. The combination of products or associated businesses creates a value that would not exist if the parts were separated. Synergies can provide a unique package of products and service that enhances the experience. A café can offer a catering service from its existing kitchen. A bakery can be a retailer and wholesaler. There have been a number of garden centres that have opened successful cafés. Currently there is a trend to establish small cafés in quality book stores.

Franchise. Franchises offer opportunities to people who wish to be associated with someone else's great idea. Good franchises can cost a lot of money but you are buying another organisation's intellectual property and their ability to turn your investment into profit. When you are stuck for ideas, a franchise is always worth considering but you will need to get good legal and business advice to evaluate whether it is a sound investment.

MARKET SEGMENTATION: THE KEY TO SUCCESS. Market segments are defined as groups of customers with similar or distinct needs and characteristics. *Segmentation* assesses the product, its purpose and relationship to the customer. It provides a key to success for all businesses.

It is easy to bundle every customer into the generic category of *customers*. By doing this, you forgo the opportunity to understand the different types of customers that you have and their specific needs. Concentrating on just one segment can leave you exposed if that segment disappears. For your hospitality business to succeed you will need more than one market segment to focus on. Having said that, you need to be aware that you cannot be all things to all people and there will come a point where you need to limit the choice of segments. What is intriguing is that as you learn to understand the distinctive needs of each segment, new opportunities become apparent.

In the hospitality industry there are many market segments. The bigger the company, the better they understand the importance of market segmentation. McDonald's offers inexpensive, fast meals that cater for people in a hurry or on a budget. McDonald's understands the nuances of marketing. To attract different segments, McDonald's has evolved chicken burgers and fish products. Now they are targeting the coffee-café market with McCafé. In the 1980s Kentucky Fried Chicken recognised a change in the motivations of its customers and renamed itself KFC. By doing this customers became less focused on the possible negative "fried" food aspect. Millbrook, the Queenstown resort, offers luxury accommodation with excellent food and wine facilities and a golf course of an international standard. Many people travel the world for golf and seek out new, exotic locations.

Successful smaller hospitality businesses are also aware of their market segments. L'Affare, the Wellington coffee establishment, offers good coffee, excellent café style food and a child-friendly environment. It roasts and wholesales its own coffee and retails coffee machines and accessories. Early mornings are a popular time as Wellington workers walk to work, stopping off for a latte at 7.15am. In Christchurch this market barely exists as virtually everyone drives to work. When L'Affare ceased to trade on Sundays for lifestyle reasons, an uproar was felt around Wellington. The Sunday brunch diners, which in Wellington are a large, lucrative market, had to be content to venture elsewhere to other cafés around the city.

How to segment a market. There are many ways to segment groups of customers with similar or distinct needs and characteristics. The first step is to identify the similarity of customer needs within the segment and to look for unmet needs. The size of the market and its potential for growth also need to be considered. In the box below are some methods by which to segment a market.

> **MARKET SEGMENTS**
> 1. **Demographics.** Age, sex, marital status, family, race, nationality and religion. *"I want to appeal to married Maori women under 40."*
> 2. **Occupation.** Clubs and professional associations, such as lawyers, accountants, doctors, nurses, teachers, etc.
> 3. **Income.** *"I don't care how much it costs, I just want it!"*
> 4. **Geographic location.** Is it possible to expand your successful formula to another area? Is it possible to choose a location where there is no competition?
> 5. **Brand loyalty.** Do they buy your product because of the brand? For example, Crabtree and Evelyn, Fortnum and Mason, Fauchon, etc.
> 6. **International Tourists.** What market do you target? North America, Germany, UK, Australia, Japan, Hong Kong, Malaysia, etc. How do you meet their diverse needs?

Psychographics. Psychographics is also a means to market segmentation. This term is used to describe the lifestyle, interests, attitudes, opinions and behaviour of different market segments. As consumers become more affluent their preferences change. Lifestyle issues become more influential in determining choice. Convenience and ease are important considerations for busy people. Attitudes change, as demonstrated by the uproar over genetically modified crops. From organic eggs to organic cotton, a change in attitude affects demand.

EXAMPLES OF PSYCHOGRAPHICS ARE:
1. Culinary tastes. *What do I feel like eating?*

"I wish to eat food that I would not prepare at home, such as Thai, Malay, Vietnamese, Chinese, Indian or Japanese. I also like vegetarian food, pizza, and fish and chips."

2. Wine Focus.

"I wish to bring my own wine."
"I wish to be able to choose from an extensive list of New Zealand wines."
"I only want to dine at a place that has Italian wines."

3. Entertainment.

"I would like to enjoy live music while I dine."
"I would like to dance tonight."
"I seek out places that offer Latin dancing."

4. Food as a destination.

"I will drive all over town to seek out the product."
"I've come to your restaurant because of your reputation for quality."
"I've come to try your famous dish."
"I buy only organic foods."
"I'm always looking for new places to go."
"I like to go for a leisurely Sunday drive in the country and finish at a nice place for lunch."

An example of market segmentation is given below. The chart demonstrates how you can segment a market according to age. For a young family who are interested in fast service and a simple inexpensive menu, the selection of beers and wine may not be important. For a couple in their 50s who are out for a dining experience, the menu and selection of wines may be very important, and the price irrelevant. Trying to cater for both these markets at the same time can cause confusion and neither group is satisfied. The segments are endless. Some can be regarded as *"un-cool"* like the over-55-year market. Christchurch Casino offers this group a *"Golden oldies"* $2 lunch on Mondays and Tuesdays to target this lucrative niche.

Segmentation: Breaking down the market into different groups of customers

	Family	Family	Adults	Adults	Adults	Adults	Adults
Age	kids under 10	kids 11–17 yrs	18–24 yrs	25–34 yrs	35–49 yrs	50–65 yrs	65 yrs +
Menu selection	simple	simple	standard	standard	gourmet	gourmet	standard
Quality of food	yes	yes	yes	yes	yes	yes	yes
Portion size	small	normal/large	normal/large	normal	normal	normal	small
Price of menu	sensitive	sensitive	sensitive	no	no	no	no
Service delivery	fast	fast	no rush	no rush	no rush	no rush	no rush
Service quality	yes	yes	yes	yes	yes	yes	yes
Something for the kids to do	yes	yes	no	no	no	no	no
Wine selection	no	no	no	no	yes	yes	no
Price of wine	sensitive	sensitive	sensitive	no	no	no	no
Beer selection	no	no	yes	no	no	no	no
Price of beer	no	no	yes				
Non-alcoholic beverages	yes	yes	no	no	no	no	no
Quality of coffee	no	yes	yes	yes	yes	yes	yes
Price of coffee	sensitive	no	no	no	no	no	no
Facilities	high chair		bar				
Decor	no	no	no	yes	yes	yes	yes
Noisy	yes	yes	yes	yes	no	no	no
Ambience	no	no	no	yes	yes	yes	yes
Music	loud	loud	loud	backg'd	backg'd	backg'd	backg'd
Cleanliness	yes	no	no	yes	yes	yes	yes

Once you have determined a number of segments to focus on, the next question to ask is, *"Which segments will be the biggest?"* One of the challenges you may find is when the biggest market segment is not the most profitable. At Hay's we had a large market of muffin and sandwich buyers purchasing a muffin for $1.50 and a sandwich for $4. While these people came every day and were valued regulars, they did not buy anything else from us and we needed a staff member to service this particular segment. Because the sandwiches were cheap and delicious, they were popular, and even if we sold 20 muffins and 30 sandwiches, we still could have ended up with sales of less than $200. Dropping our biggest segment of regulars was a difficult choice but a sandwich service was no longer part of our vision.

UNDERSTANDING THE MARKET. It is easy to run off the management buzz words such as competitive advantage and synergies. Actually achieving them takes understanding, time and energy. Having a good idea must be backed up with evidence that it *is* a good idea. You cannot hope to create an on-going competitive advantage without understanding the market that you are in and especially with whom you will compete. To be successful, the first step is to determine what you are trying to achieve. The second step is to seek out businesses that you feel are successful and evaluate how they operate.

By observing, you can learn a great deal. Many people do work experience or *stagière*, where they are allowed to do unpaid work or observe in a restaurant or kitchen. It is regarded as an opportunity to experience the service as it happens.

In New Zealand, we are very poor at conducting meaningful market research. New entrants to the hospitality industry are some of the worst. Yes, they observe a successful business and then decide to imitate it. Many fail to appreciate what is actually involved in being successful. The casual professionalism of a well trained waiter is deceptive as it just looks easy. I am regularly disturbed by the confidence of the ill-informed. When appraising a business idea, it is important to retain a healthy detachment. One of the options must always be the *"Do nothing"* where you walk away from the proposal. Think of the wise adage, *"Fold the money twice and put it back in your pocket"*.

S.W.O.T. This analysis is the traditional tool that is used to evaluate an idea, a product or a business. It provides a simple but very effective framework. It is useful not only at the initial stage of any project, but also as a strategic planning tool. Each year at Hay's, we have a strategic planning meeting where we conduct a S.W.O.T. analysis of the organisation. It has become one of our tools for change.

> **S.W.O.T.[4]** *can be defined as an analysis of:*
> **Strengths and weaknesses**
> This looks at the business, its management, resources and products. These are internal issues and are therefore within the control of the business. This analysis helps to determine whether the business has the ability to exploit any opportunities detected.
> **Opportunities and threats**
> This is information on the competition, customers and other aspects of the environment external to the business. This helps to identify opportunities to meet customer needs and it also helps to discern threats that the products or business might face.

David Aaker in his book *Strategic Market Management*[5] expands on the S.W.O.T. and calls this analysis *External Analysis*. This considers a comprehensive range of areas that need to be investigated when making a business assessment. Four of these areas which are discussed below.

CUSTOMER ANALYSIS. It is essential to understand your customers and be clear about who they are. The riddle is to achieve this while still being open to new ideas and different customer motivations.

Who will be your customers?
- How will you meet their needs?
- Is there a genuine need?
- Why should people buy your products/service?
- Will people understand your products/service?
- Will you need to build a market?

Customer Motivation. Understanding what motivates your customers is essential. The closer you look at a market the more you become aware of the different motivations of groups of customers.

What aspects of your product do customers value most?
- Are they price sensitive?
- Will they be motivated by discounts?
- Do they come only because you are BYO?
- Do they come because you have the facilities to cater for big bookings?
- Would they come more often if you developed a reward system for loyalty?
- How will you attract new customers?
- Why are some customers dissatisfied?
- How often are customers dissatisfied?
- What problems do they identify with your service?

MARKET ANALYSIS. Market analysis determines the attractiveness, in terms of profit potential, of a market to current and potential entrants. When assessing a market it is important to consider where your product will sit and if there is a genuine demand.

Identify where your product sits in the market place.
- What is happening in the market?
- Is the market well supplied?
- Are the suppliers profitable?
- How good is your product?
- Is there a real demand for your product?
- Is it unique and special?
- Will customers flock to your door to try it?
- What do you offer that they cannot get elsewhere?
- Is it a commodity? For example, muffins, tomato sandwiches, burgers or fish and chips.

- Is it expensive?
- How will existing competitors react to you setting up?
- Is their level of commitment such that they will try and take you out?
- Will they drop their prices to compete?
- If they drop their prices will you still have a market?
- What are the trends?

ENVIRONMENTAL ANALYSIS. This assesses the forces outside the organisation beyond the customer. It is easy to get overwhelmed by the enormity of such an analysis; however, too often people do not research obvious constraints, such as resource consents, before they are so far into the project that it is too costly to abandon it. An environmental analysis looks at the impact of things such as government policy, technology (e.g. new rapid cook conveyer belt pizza ovens and point of sale systems), economic conditions (e.g. interest rates, exchange rates and inflation rates), cultural trends (e.g. lifestyle changes such as eating out more regularly or more frequent overseas travel) and demographic change (e.g. brain drain of young New Zealanders leaving to work and live overseas).

Government Policy and Regulation. Resource consents are administered by regional councils and local district or city councils. A check of a district or city plan for zoning issues is often the first step in the process of market research. City or district plans may preclude the establishment of the business in the intended location. This is particularly true of businesses wishing to set up in residential areas. There can be huge costs to just get through the resource consent stage especially if you have neighbours who object to your plans. It is costly and time consuming. The last thing that you want is to spend all your capital on lawyers fees!

COMPETITOR ANALYSIS. Everyone is your competitor. In the hospitality industry your competitors, in the broadest sense, can be all places selling food. Economics teaches about the threat of substitute products. *A substitute is a good that can be used in place of another good.* There are countless substitutes in this industry. They range from a consumer's decision to buy fish and chips tonight to buying a burger tomorrow and making dinner at home on Thursday. Even a person going on a diet can result in a change in demand for your product.

Understanding your competitors is important because it can provide insights into their future strategies and may enable you to predict emerging threats and opportunities. A highly committed competitor may respond to your innovation by copying you, and then pricing beneath you, in an attempt to destroy the new market for your product.

Michael Porter's *Five-Forces Model*[6] measures the attractiveness of a market in terms of long term profitability. Low prices impact on profitability and will influence whether a business chooses to stay in the market or to exit. Porter identifies five forces that influence competition:

1. *The intensity of competition* among existing firms. Intense rivalry will reduce profitability.
2. *Threat of potential entrants.* Competitors will enter if the profits are high. Will your competitive advantage be undermined?
3. *Threat of substitute products.* Can the customers choose another product?
4. *Bargaining power of customers.* Can the customers compel the business to be more competitive by forcing prices down?
5. *Bargaining power of suppliers.* A supplier may raise prices which in turn could impact on the profitability of your business.

The collective strength of the five factors determines the attractiveness of an industry and the potential for sound financial performance by influencing prices, costs and the level of capital investment required.

Cost structure. Most effective competition competes on cost. History demonstrates that as new firms enter the market they often have a cost advantage. Often their cost of equipment is less. They may however, lack the skills to compete effectively. The decision of supermarkets to operate bakeries offered them a cost advantage as they produced all their baked products on site. The Warehouse, if it decides to open a retail food division, will benefit from the fact that the business is already well established in existing locations. The commitment of the supermarkets will be tested if The Warehouse seeks to take market share from them. The Starbucks franchise is owned in New Zealand by Restaurant Brands who also own Pizza Hut and KFC. They are establishing new businesses in a well-supplied market. Their franchise costs, as well as the high set-up costs for the imported Starbucks décor and imported coffee, may undermine their ability to successfully compete against well-established owner-operated businesses with a loyal customer base.

Scarcity. Economists define competition as the contest for command over scarce resources.[7] They explain *scarcity*, as the situation where your wants, which are *unlimited*, always exceed the *limited* resources that are available to satisfy them. Scarcity forces people to make a *rational choice* and in order to do this, people must optimise by evaluating the *opportunity cost* of using their resources in a particular way. Michael Parken[8] in his book *Economics* explains, "If you cannot have everything that you want then you have to choose among the alternatives. The best thing that you choose not to do – *the alternative forgone* – is the cost of the thing that you choose to do … everything has an *opportunity cost*." For example, if you choose to go to a bar and stay up until 4.00 am when you have to work at 8.00 am, you will be feeling pretty tired. The opportunity cost of staying up late is that you will not perform well at work.

Leading wine maker, Cloudy Bay has an excellent grasp of the concept of scarcity. Each year it makes an allocation of its famous Sauvignon Blanc to wine retailers and restaurants. At Hay's we are permitted a paltry three cases. But we do not quibble. We are grateful! The scarcity creates demand and we anxiously pick up our allocation and hope the sales representative can locate an extra case. Our diners are aware of its scarcity and nod approvingly when they see it on our wine list. And then they order a bottle. If Cloudy Bay Sauvignon Blanc was readily available, the mystique would wane.

> **SCARCITY: YOU CAN'T ALWAYS GET WHAT YOU WANT!**
> - Scarcity is the foundation of economic theory.
> - Your wants are *unlimited* and always exceed the limited resources available to satisfy them.
> - Scarcity forces people to make *rational choices*; to optimise.
> - To optimise, people evaluate the cost of alternatives (*opportunity cost*), that is they evaluate the cost of using their resources in a particular way.
> - Scarcity implies competition (*a contest for command over scarce resources*).

Is competition a good thing? Competition provides consumers with a choice. It keeps businesses honest as they must constantly benchmark themselves against each other. It keeps prices down. If someone charges above the market price for a beer, customers will go elsewhere. If your product is no good, you will go out of business. If a number of businesses are located near each other, they become a destination and therefore draw a broader range of customer. The Viaduct Basin in Auckland or The Strip in Christchurch are good examples of this but there will come a point when the existing businesses would prefer that no more businesses were established or that some barriers to entry existed. To create a competitive advantage a business must be better than its rivals; however as soon as you are seen to be better, the business becomes a target for imitation.

Is a monopoly is a good thing? Given a choice, most businesses would prefer to have a monopoly. You can charge what you like as there are no substitutes. Your product is scarce and you control the supply. For years there was only one bakery-café in Akaroa. When Akaroa's population swelled in summer, people would rush in at 10.00 am to buy their bread, for they knew that by lunchtime it would all be sold. During the 1990s more food businesses set up in competition as they recognised the shortage of supply. In Nelson in the 1960s the café Chez Eelco, became an institution because it was the only place of this style. Over the years it has had to compete with numerous imitators, finally closing its doors in 2000.

When we opened Hay's Café in 1994, we were the only café along our block of Victoria Street, except for our Deli on the corner. By 1999, there were another ten businesses offering a lunch service all in competition for the same market. Over the years we endeavoured to meet the market. What we noticed most was a gradual downturn in our lunch trade. We dropped our prices and offered more sandwiches and cakes *to go*. We were experiencing what Tom Peters calls *commoditisation*⁹. Lunch on Victoria Street had become a commodity. Quality was sacrificed for price. Instead of people spending $14 on lunch, they only spent $6. There were lots of substitutes for our product and many places were happy to accept such a small sale. We were uncompetitive. Saggio di Vino, a well-established café-bar that specialised in wine, reduced its lunch trade to just Thursdays and Fridays in 1998. *"I can't stand to serve two women with a house salad and glass of water for lunch. I'd rather be closed!"* exclaimed owner Lisa Scholz.

As our dinner trade prospered and we became increasingly focused on meeting the needs of this market, our lunch became an embarrassment. The lunch experience was completely different to the dinner one. For the local Christchurch market, we were still associated with lamb burgers and souvlaki at lunchtime. At dinner we were known for Canterbury lamb, raised at our Pigeon Bay property. We became the *lamb experience* for the constant stream of international tourists. The Rack of Lamb at $29 was our best selling meal. By January 2000 we too had abandoned the lunch trade.

This discussion underlies two economic principles, the law of demand and the law of supply.

Using the example above, you could say that the price of lunch at Hay's was higher than the price at other establishments. There was a range of substitutes available. The average consumer did not want to spend so much of his or her scarce income on lunch and preferred something of lesser quality. In Christchurch the size of the lunch time population around Victoria Street is static, so when we lost some customers, there was not a pool of other customers to replace them. Demand for our lunch product dropped.

Threat of new entrants. In the mid 1990s, when people were looking to invest in hospitality businesses, they turned to Victoria Street, a city location close to the Christchurch Casino, three hotels, Convention Centre, and an assortment of businesses. This is a good location. In terms of servicing this market there was Hay's on Victoria (the old Preservatory Kilmore), Hay's Café and the Jolly Poacher. At 3.00 am, if you were up, the Jolly Poacher was rocking. The area was perceived to be profitable and therefore attractive for investment. More hospitality businesses were established and as a result the market share of the existing businesses was undermined. This was an example of the law of supply.

The impact of the increase in suppliers of hospitality resulted in an increase in the quantity of food or beverage supplied. There was more choice for the consumer. This in turn forced a drop in price because the consumer was able to choose from cheaper alternatives, particularly for coffee and lunch.

The establishment of The Strip in Christchurch, like The Viaduct Basin in Auckland, happened at an unbelievable pace. Potential investors were impressed at the apparent success of Coyotes and Espresso 124. They saw how busy the Jolly Poacher was with its 24-hour licence. Within eighteen months, all the retail space in Oxford Terrace, between Hereford and Cashel Streets had been converted to café-bars. The expansion then spread to retail space under the Clarendon Towers that had been untenanted for nearly ten years. Like Victoria Street, The Strip was experiencing a phenomenon similar to *perfect competition*.

> **Perfect competition occurs:**
> 1. When *many firms* sell identical products and there are many buyers.
> 2. When there are *price takers* who cannot influence the price of a product and therefore have to accept the price.
> 3. When there are *no barriers to entry* so that anyone can set up a business.
> 4. When there is *full information* so that the market is informed about all the prices of all the firms.

Until 1989, there were legislative barriers to entry which made it difficult to get a liquor licence. When John McCormack wished to open Mansfield House in Christchurch, he bought a licence from a Southland pub that had closed down. He then had to face a court case where a brewery challenged the granting of the licence to operate in Christchurch. Mansfield House went on to be one of the first café-bars that are so common today. Since the legislation change in 1989, the only real barriers to entry for a hospitality business are town planning issues.

In some industries the cost of financing the investment can be a barrier to entry. Logically, this should be the case with small investors in the wine industry and latterly the olive industry. If we consider the cost of land, grape plantings and setting up a winemaking facility, added to the fact that the grower must wait seven years until full production is reached, it would seem that there are significant barriers to entry. However, like food, wine has captured investors' imagination. In time, many of the small wineries will not survive and their only means of making a return on their investment will be to sell to a bigger player. In many cases this will ironically be the competitor that they sought to compete with in the first place.

Shutdown. The decision to close Hay's during the day is an example of a *shutdown* point. We had reached the point where the maximum profit we could achieve was the same regardless of whether we were open or shut. In fact it cost us money to remain open. The opportunity cost of remaining open was substantial. The skills of the staff employed to service this segment could be used more productively for something else.

Work Sheet: The following work sheet will help you to evaluate your competitors and understand what makes them successful.

APPRAISING YOUR COMPETITORS

Rank out of 5 with 1 being bad and 5 being excellent	1 Bad	2	3	4	5 Excellent

Menu selection

A)	Price of menu	1	2	3	4	5
B)	Quality of food	1	2	3	4	5
C)	Portion size	1	2	3	4	5
D)	Consistency of food served	1	2	3	4	5

Drinks selection

E)	Price of wine	1	2	3	4	5
F)	Variety of wine	1	2	3	4	5
G)	Beer selection	1	2	3	4	5
H)	Price of beer	1	2	3	4	5
I)	Non-alcoholic beverages	1	2	3	4	5
J)	Coffee	1	2	3	4	5
K)	Price of coffee	1	2	3	4	5
L)	Quality of coffee	1	2	3	4	5

Service delivery

M)	Service quality	1	2	3	4	5
N)	Service attitude	1	2	3	4	5
O)	Motivation	1	2	3	4	5
P)	Staff turnover	1	2	3	4	5

Decor

Q)	Ambience	1	2	3	4	5
R)	Music	1	2	3	4	5
S)	Other facilities	1	2	3	4	5
T)	Cleanliness	1	2	3	4	5

Marketing

U)	Branding of business	1	2	3	4	5
V)	Advertising/ promotional budget	1	2	3	4	5
W)	Innovation	1	2	3	4	5

Customer Base

X)	Market share	1	2	3	4	5
Y)	Loyalty	1	2	3	4	5

- Maximum score 125 points.
- A competitor scoring over 100 should be regarded as a serious threat and the proposal reconsidered.
- A competitor scoring 80–99 is a potential threat.
- A competitor scoring under 79 is not regarded as a threat.

Formal Market Research. Market research is the collection of information about a proposal which enables you to make an informed decision. It helps you to understand the market and evaluate it. It also assesses the organisation and its ability to perform. As the power has shifted from the producer to the customer, businesses have discovered the wisdom of finding out more about their customers and their motivations.

Information is everywhere. If you want to start researching a proposal there is a lot of information available to help you. Ensuring that it is relevant and valid is a more difficult prospect. You can spend a long time at the library researching and in the end be no better informed! The Department of Statistics is the source of much information, drawing from the five-yearly census and annual surveys, on topics such as employment and household spending. Organisations such as the New Zealand Employers and local Chamber of Commerce also collect information that they make available to their members. Publications, trade associations and local authorities are also repositories for information. Often this information is historical and may no longer be relevant. There comes a point when you need to get out and see for yourself exactly what is happening in the market and where you propose to establish.

Observation. Observation is the simplest form of research. You can tell a lot about what people are thinking by their behaviour and body language. If someone sits down at a table, looks at your menu and then gets up and walks out, it will probably indicate that they did not like the menu or your prices. By observing people's body language, you can tell whether they are happy or not.

Primary information is gathered when you undertake field research. This could take the form of a site survey with customer counts taken over a period. It could be a questionnaire that you ask members of the public or your existing customers to complete. A market research company could conduct the survey on your behalf.

Surveys. When conducting a survey it is vital to understand the purpose of the research. Is to find out what people think about your product? Is it to monitor how your customers feel? Is it to find out more about the demographic mix of the passing population? Surveys can provide an insight into the thinking of your customers and prospective customers.

In this age of customer information we are rapidly becoming *surveyed out*. Complex and time-consuming surveys, while offering the business a wealth of information, have become a nuisance and an invasion of privacy for the consumer. Often surveys are only effective because the respondent is rewarded with a prize or enters a draw for a product. *Mail surveys* require a freepost envelope to be effective. *Personal interviews* can be conducted by standing on a corner and randomly approaching people. It is important not to ask too many questions as the respondent will get impatient. Around 3–6 short, well-worded questions are sufficient. In *telephone interviews* the same standards apply. *Fax surveys* can be difficult to get responses from. Currently the *internet* is a successful medium for surveys as the technology is new and people seem more willing to respond.

Validity. In order to ensure that your survey is valid you must be consistent in your approach. To understand the trends and make a fair prediction you need to survey over a period of time. One day is not sufficient. This may mean that for two weeks you are up at 7.00am each morning to assess the people-flow and evaluate the breakfast potential for a site. Each day you must evaluate the same set of criteria. You must also be aware of your own biases and inability to see what is before you. In Victoria Street, we are located opposite the Christchurch Casino. Numerous people have commented to me over the years about our excellent location. It comes as a shock when I tell them that we get very little business from Casino patrons. The Casino caters for all their needs such as food, drinks and entertainment. It is fully self-contained and when the patrons leave they have spent their money.

It is easy to devise a set of questions that you wish answered. The best questions start with the words: *What, Why, When, How, Where* and *Who*. These questions are general and will often let a respondent give more information. *Leading* questions force the respondent to answer in a particular way. Questions starting with *Did, Do* and *Are* often fall into this category.

Leading questions	**Open questions**
"Do you like to drink coffee?"	*"What do you like to drink?"*
"Are you a regular customer?"	*"How often do you eat here?"*
"Did you see the advertisement?"	*"Where did you hear about us?"*

Samples of surveys that you may wish to carry out.

1. **Objective: To evaluate the customer-flow past the proposed location to determine the hours that the business should open**
   - Method   Site survey by observation to determine the demographics (age, sex) of those passing by
   - By whom   Self
   - Cost   No cost, own time
   - Hours of the   7.00am–9.00am   12.00am–2.00pm
     survey   4.00pm–6.00pm   9.00pm–11.00pm

2. **Objective: To evaluate existing customers' response to a proposed change in hours**
   - Method   Mail survey
   - By whom   Post to customers on the mailing list with a freepost reply
   - Cost   Collating time, photocopies and postage

3. **Objective: To evaluate the menu and wine list**
   - Method   Questionnaire
   - By whom   Given to customers when they have finished their meal
   - Cost   Collating time and photocopies

4. **To evaluate how many people travel to Picton**
   - Method   Telephone survey
   - By whom   Professional market research firm
   - Cost $5000–10,000

The survey below is an example of a simple survey designed to give customer feedback about new proposals as well as existing products and service. Respondents are asked for some personal information to help build a profile about the types of customers frequenting the business.

HAY'S ON VICTORIA CUSTOMER SURVEY

Hay's On Victoria is committed to providing superior service for you. We would welcome your responses to this questionnaire and other comments that you may have.

Please indicate by circling the appropriate response below.

1. Hay's On Victoria is proposing to extend the opening hours by remaining open until 10.00pm. Would you take advantage of this?

   No   **Don't know**   **Yes**

2. Are you aware that Hay's On Victoria is open on Saturday and Sunday?

   No   **Yes**

3. Have you ever taken advantage of Hay's On Victoria's weekend opening?

   No   **Yes**

4. How satisfied are you with the quality of service provided?

   1   **2**   **3**   **4**   **5**   **6**   **7**

   Poor   **Excellent**

5. How important is speed of service to you?

   1   **2**   **3**   **4**   **5**   **6**   **7**

   Of little importance   **Extremely important**

8. What foods would you like to see available?

   ....

   ....

9. Are you aware that Hay's provides a catering service?

   No   **Yes**

General Comments..

....

....

Thank you for your participation in this customer survey.
We would be grateful if you would provide the following information.

Sex: Female Male

Age: Under 20 20–30 30–40 40–50 50+

Area of residence in Christchurch ....

Other than Christchurch..

When completing this survey are you:

On holiday **Working** **Shopping** **Socialising**

Other...

1. Covey, S. *The 7 Habits of Highly Effective People*, 1989.
2. Oster, S. *Modern Competitor Analysis*, 1999.
3. Schultz, H. *Pour your heart into it*, 1997.
4. Assael, H *Marketing Principles and Strategy* 2nd ed., 1993.
5   Aaker, D. *Strategic Market Management*, 4th *ed.*, 1995.
6. Porter, M. *Competitive Strategy*, 1980.
7. Parken, M. *Economics*, 1990.
8. Parken, M. *Economics*, 1990.
9. Peters, T, *The Circle of Innovation*, 1997.

CHAPTER FOUR

SETTING UP –
KNOWING THOSE COSTS

T his chapter addresses some issues that you need to consider before the doors actually open. The planning stage is often characterised by excitement and hope, but tempered by the harsh reality of costs and compliance. Understanding some fundamental accounting principles and key hospitality performance ratios will help you to evaluate how the business will fulfil your expectations. This chapter includes a discussion on legal issues and introduces key legislation that affects hospitality businesses.

To any entrepreneur, I would offer this advice:
Once you've figured out what you want to do, find
someone who has done it before. Find not just talented
executives but even more experienced entrepreneurs
and businesspeople who can guide you. ... If they share
your values and aspirations, and if they freely share
their counsel, they can help you through rough patches
and celebrate your victories as their own. ... And
with the right mentor don't be afraid to expose your
vulnerabilities. Admit you don't know what you don't
know. When you acknowledge your weaknesses and
ask for advice, you'll be surprised how much others
will help.

Howard Schultz,
Pour Your Heart Into It.

LEGAL STRUCTURE. In Chapter Three, we talked of establishing a vision for the business. By inference what I described was a vision of one person. However often, businesses are run by more than one person. Partnerships can offer synergies that an individual owner struggles to achieve alone. They may open avenues for finance and skills and enable the business to expand and grow at a much faster rate. What is important is to go into business with people who share the same vision and commitment to work.

Many hospitality partnerships are born over a drink in a dark corner of a pub or restaurant. It may be the Friday night drink after your chef's course or the celebration dinner following graduation. Inspired by the congenial surroundings or the lack of it, people rise to the challenge by saying *"I could do this better"* or *"I've always wanted to do this…"*. One of the first traps that a prospective owner can fall into is the *ad hoc* agreement to form a business relationship with people whom, given a different set of circumstances, you would never find yourself attached to.

Business partnerships with more than two people are much harder to make successful. The individuals may bring different skills and money to the business, but gaining consensus on the direction of the business can be difficult. Decision-making can be laborious. One person cannot decide without the consent of the others. Every meeting becomes a committee meeting. Over time factions appear and conflict arises. Often the only solution is to sell the business or disband the partnership.

The key to a successful partnership is to have established some sort of structure at the outset. This should set out the roles and responsibilities of the partners, explain how decisions will be made and preferably set out the process of dissolving the partnership while the partners are still friends and talking. It is important to get professional advice at this point. Attention to these details at the beginning may alleviate a lot of problems and costs later on. There are two main forms of legal structure: a company formed under The Companies Act or a partnership, under The Partnership Act.

Forming a company. While I talked in the previous paragraphs about partnerships, most businesses use the limited liability company as the legal structure for their business. In law the company is a separate entity from the people who:

- own it (the shareholders)
- decide how it should operate (the directors)
- work for it (the workers)

The company limits the liability of the shareholders unlike a partnership where the partners are each personally and jointly liable for *all* the debts and liabilities of the business. However even with the company format, as soon as you sign a personal guarantee, all liability for the obligations covered by the guarantee reverts to you personally. It is important to gain sound professional advice to work through the options for establishing your businesses.

Professional advisors. You will need to engage a lawyer and an accountant. The more you understand about the issues that they deal with, the more confident you will be in discussing their recommendations. You will use a lawyer during the set-up stage to form the company and to draft shareholder agreements and loan documents for the bank or financier. A lawyer will also negotiate the lease or purchase agreement as well as advise on general questions of compliance. If all things go well, you may not need to visit the lawyer again for several years. What is important is that you find a lawyer who specialises in commercial law and can demonstrate a record of establishing similar businesses. Your old school friend who is a sole practitioner, specialising in family law, is not a good choice. This option may appear to be cheaper but you will not get the same quality of advice that a commercial lawyer would give.

Your accountant will need to see you at least once a year when completing the annual set of accounts and filing a tax return. An accountant should be able to provide you with information about how the business is performing. The advent of the spreadsheet has revolutionised how information is gathered and has liberated the lay person from dependence on an accountant. With a little training you should be able to understand how to use a spreadsheet to monitor your business. The more you know about these matters, the better you will understand the business. Remember to always discuss the fees for the job and where possible get a quote from the lawyer or accountant before they commence work.

Legal compliance. To be competent, a manager must have an overview of the legislation that affects business in New Zealand. The legislation provides a safety net for both the employer and employee. It is important for a manager to take specific advice when an issue arises. It may save you a lot of anxiety later on.

Laws are made in two ways. *Acts of Parliament* (statutes) make law. This process involves the introduction of a *Bill* by a Member of Parliament or the Government. There are three readings before Parliament votes and the successful *Bill* is sent to the Governor General for royal assent. *Judge-made-laws* are the rules of law made by judges presiding in the courts. These laws set a legal precedent that future judges and lawyers will refer to and must follow if similar cases arise again. These laws are referred to as *case law* or the *common law*, and have accumulated over the centuries.

New Zealand's Judicial System consists of

Privy Council (London)

Court of Appeal

High Court (major court cases: large commercial disputes, murder, manslaughter, drugs)

District Court (civil and criminal cases under $200,000)
Disputes Tribunal (under $12,000)

Employment Court   Environment Court   Family Court

Contracts. Contracts are legal obligations that are agreed between the parties involved thereby creating a legal relationship between them. The terms of the relationship are defined and once accepted, the conditions are binding, even if money or goods have not been exchanged. There are few rules to determine whether or not a contract must be in writing. *Written contacts,* such as an agreement to lease a building, set out the conditions of lease. Signing of the document signals acceptance. A *Verbal contract* such as an agreement to supply a service can be less specific. For many businesses verbal contracts are common and firms often rely on a verbal contracts even with major customers. If the relationship breaks down, it can be difficult to determine the original intent of the agreement. One party's interpretation of the contract often differs from the other's. This also can occur when there is a written contract. Many contracts will include mechanisms, such as mediation and arbitration, to resolve disputes.

Once the agreement has been made, generally it may only be negated if it is illegal. This situation can arise if a contract breaks other laws, or if one of the parties is a minor, mentally infirm or, in some circumstances, intoxicated when accepting the agreement. Lack of genuine consent can result if there is evidence of duress, misrepresentation or a genuine mistake. Disputes are common in business and managers must be very careful before entering into a contract that is legally binding. Appropriate advice should be sought.

Personal Guarantees. Personal Guarantees are an onerous reality of business today. It is common to find that even your small suppliers will want you to sign a personal guarantee. This means that you will be *personally liable* for any unpaid debts of the business. Financial institutions and landlords will also require personal guarantees. Leases can present a particularly scary prospect in the future. If you sell the business and assign the lease to a new owner and then the business fails, the landlord can come back to you for the rent and expenses. In some situations the lease can revert back. A well-known Christchurch restaurateur, Görge Spiteri, experienced this three years after he had left his Hereford Street restaurant; fortunately, he was happy to resume the lease. Always take legal advice first so that you understand the full consequence of signing. A lawyer may be able to suggest ways of limiting the liability. The rule with personal guarantees is *do not sign them unless you really really have to.*

SUMMARY OF LEGISLATION. This list is designed to give an overview of the legislation and is in no way comprehensive. The internet has numerous sites which offer free information on legislation. Major law firms like Buddle Findlay www.budfin.co.nz and Chapman Tripp www.chapmantripp.co.nz are a good place to start. The Government's website www.govt.nz contains a wealth of information from policy statements to recent press releases.

Companies Act 1993. The Companies Act sets out the business practices that companies and directors of companies must abide by. It lists how to form a company, the constitution and certain tests of insolvency. The Registrar approves names for companies. Look up www.companies.govt.nz.

Commerce Act 1986. This Act promotes competition between businesses and looks to protect the community against anti-competitive practices. In 1999, the Commerce Commission, the authority charged with overseeing the Act, brought a number of successful actions against businesses. For example, three North Island meat processors were fined for price setting because they colluded to set the price paid for meat.

The Fair Trading Act 1986. This Act protects people against unfair business practices. It prohibits businesses from misleading or deceiving the public with particular regard to advertising. The Commerce Commission's website www.comcom.govt.nz has comprehensive information about the Commerce Act and the Fair Trading Act.

Sale of Goods Act 1908 and Personal Property Securities Act 1999. This Sale of Goods Act covers basic laws relating to the sale of goods and how to determine ownership of an title to them. It has recently been supplemented by the *Personal Property Securities Act 1999* which relates to security interests in personal property such as romalpa clauses.

Consumer Guarantees Act 1993. This Act protects consumers from accepting products that do not fulfill the customer's expectations. The Ministry of Consumer Affairs website www.consumer-ministry.govt.nz contains information about your obligations.

Intellectual Property. The control of intellectual property is protected under a number of statutes as well as the common law:
• Trade Marks Act 1953
• Patents Act 1953
• Copyrights Act 1994

   Passing-off is to claim that a product or service is not what it seems. This is a *tort* or civil wrong and is governed by the common law.

Resource Management Act 1991. This Act sets out how the environment should be protected. The Act is administered partly by the local city or district councils, and for issues such as discharges to air and water, by the regional councils.

Local Body By-laws. City and district councils administer environmental health and the Building Act. Failure to follow the required approvals can result in breaches of the regulations. Your local council should be able to give you this information. Amongst other things the regulations include that:
• all kitchen floors must be *coved* with the lino curved up the wall.
• kitchen benches must have up-stands to prevent dirt building up where the bench meets that wall.
• there should be one hand basin for every ten food handlers.

   Consents or approvals may be required for:

   • A change of use. This is when you are conducting a different type of business to the one that was previously there.
   • Outdoor seating.
   • Gardens and some types of plantings.
   • Parking. You may be required to provide a number of car parks.
   • Dangerous goods (e.g. gas).
   • Serving food. For example, an environmental health licence to operate a food premises includes the number of patrons expected and interesting things like the number of air changes per hour.
   • A liquor licence.
   • Signage. There are restrictions on size and location.
   • Building upgrades under the Building Act 1991.

Human Rights Act 1993. It is illegal to discriminate on grounds of sex, marital status, religious or ethical belief, race, colour, ethnic or national origins, disability, age, political opinion, employment status, family status or sexual orientation.

Privacy Act 1993. This Act controls how personal information is to be collected and used. Information must be collected for a lawful purpose.
- The person must agree or the information must be public.
- The person must be aware who will hold the information.
- The organisation must ensure against loss, unauthorised access or misuse.
- The organisation cannot keep personal information for longer than it is required.
- A person is entitled to have access to the information held about him/her.
- Requests to have the information corrected must be granted.
- The organisation must ensure that personal information is accurate and not misleading.
- Information collected for one purpose is not to be used for another.
- The organisation cannot give that information to anyone else unless that was the part of the reason for its collection.
- An organisation must not use personal identification numbers unless this is absolutely essential.

Health and Safety in Employment Act 1992. With the introduction of this Act, the responsibilities for health and safety devolved to the employer. Visit their website at the Department of Labour www.dol.govt.nz or www.osh.dol.govt.nz. Key points are noted below.
- Identify existing and new hazards and determine whether they are significant.
- Take all practical steps to eliminate, isolate or minimise hazards.
- Keep a register or written record of accidents.
- Be proactive by providing training to ensure an accident-free work place.
- Infringements may make a company liable for fines of up to $100,000 or imprisonment of not more than one year.

EMPLOYMENT LEGISLATION.
The laws that govern the employment relationship are currently under review. The Department of Labour www.dol.govt.nz has a comprehensive website which covers current legislation and the proposed changes. Acts which impact on an employer include:

Holidays Act 1981. Employees are entitled to five days special leave after six months for sickness, illness or bereavement. They must be paid for statutory holidays and receive three weeks paid holiday or 6% of their gross earnings.

Parental Leave and Employment Protection Act 1987. This Act is soon to be changed. Currently an employee is entitled to one year unpaid parental leave.

Minimum Wage Act 1983. This Act sets out the minimum wage paid to employees.

The Wages Protection Act 1983. Employees must be paid in cash, by cheque or by direct credit. Deductions from wages cannot be made without the consent of the employee.

Equal Pay Act 1972. This Act forbids discrimination in rates of pay on the grounds of gender.

Income Tax Act 1994. This Act sets out taxation obligations.

ACCOUNTING INFORMATION. Whether you are in the role of owner or manager, you must have some understanding of basic accountancy. While a business does not need to be profitable in every period, cash is the lifeblood of the business and without it in the long-run the business will fail. A business must generate sufficient profits to satisfy the needs of the owners (shareholders) and to ensure there are sufficient funds to maintain or expand the operation.

A business must be *viable*. This means that it must be able to meet its obligations as they fall due. It must retain sufficient cash *(liquidity)* to meet these commitments. *Cash is king*. Unless there is sufficient cash, a business will be forced to cease trading even though it may profitable.

Accounting information should be used as a basis for making decisions. Historical performance can show trends and help to predict future outcomes. To be useful, the information must be relevant. Relying on a set of accounts produced annually eight months after the period has ended helps no-one. Relevant and timely information is essential for a business to prosper. It helps to determine:
- the price of goods and services
- the quantity of goods and services that need to be produced or sold to break even
- the stock level
- the cost of the investment in new equipment
- financial requirements to maintain or expand the business

Management Accounting. Management accounting is internal information provided for the managers of the business. All management accounts can be produced using a spreadsheet or accounting software and enable a business manager to assess the information day to day. This can include issues such as costing, cashflows, stocktakes and calculating efficiency ratios that are used to evaluate how the business is performing.

Financial Accounting. Financial accounting is information that is provided to other interested stakeholders such as shareholders and bankers. It is a summary of the performance of the business and is usually produced by an accountant on your behalf. This consists of *the balance sheet* (statement of financial position) which provides a *snapshot* of how the business is performing on a particular day of the year *(balance date)*. It lists the assets, liabilities and owner's equity in the business. The *income statement* (often called *profit and loss* or *statement of financial performance*) illustrates the revenue that has been received and how it has been spent *(expenses)*. A business is always treated as a separate entity to the individuals running it. If the business is solvent and able to pay its debts as they fall due it will be treated as a *going concern*. This assumes that the business will continue to exist in future accounting periods.

Revenues less **Expenses** equal **Profit (Loss)**

Assets are things owned by a business that have an expected future benefit.

Fixed (capital) assets last longer than one year and in a hospitality business are essential to creating revenue. A café could not open if it did not have a coffee machine or refrigerator for the milk. Other examples include land, buildings, fixtures and fittings, equipment (pots, linen, cutlery and crockery). The value of the assets is *depreciated (the amount of benefit used up)* over the anticipated life of the asset during an accounting period. Maximum rates of depreciation are set by Inland Revenue.

Current Assets are expected to be converted into cash within one year. These include cash, debtors *(accounts receivable)*, stock *(inventory)* and prepaid expenses *(where you have paid an expense in advance, such as insurance)*.

Intangible Assets are non-physical assets, such as good will, copyright and franchise agreements.

Expenses can be described as benefits that are used up. They can be divided into different groups depending on the information required.

Operating Expenses include advertising, cleaning and rubbish, laundry, consultants, licences, vehicle, power, protective clothing, repairs and maintenance, repairs and replacements, security and uniforms.

Administration Expenses include accounting, bank charges, insurance, legal advice, office, printing and stationery, rent, staff training and the telephone.

Fixed Costs do not vary as the sales/revenue changes. These include rent, rates, insurance, wages to pay key staff, interest on term loans, licences and depreciation.

Variable Costs change in direct proportion to a change in the volume of sales/revenue. These include food purchases, wages, advertising, cleaning and rubbish, laundry, consultants, vehicle, protective clothing, security, printing and stationery, repairs and maintenance, interest on overdrafts, bank charges, power and telephone.

Cost of Goods Sold (COGS) = Cost of Sales. In a hospitality business, COGS relates to the food and beverage purchases. Some businesses will also include labour in this figure. Many small businesses bundle the food and beverage totals together. However to make the cost of goods sold more meaningful, it is better to separate the food costs from the beverage costs. To do this you also need to separate both sources of income and be able to calculate the revenue generated by your food sales and beverage sales. The **Contribution margin** is the margin that remains after the cost of goods sold has been deducted from the total sales or revenue. This is also referred to as the **Gross Profit**.

> **Gross Profit** equals **total sales** or revenue *less* **cost of goods sold** (food and beverage purchases).
> **Net Profit** equals **total sales** or revenue *less* **total expenses** (food, beverage, labour, etc).

Stock Valuation. A stocktake must be held at least once during the year and this generally occurs on the *balance date*. Businesses in the hospitality industry carry out stocktakes regularly to obtain data on gross profit/cost of goods sold as well to monitor *shrinkage* (theft). Stocktakes can be conducted weekly, bi-weekly, monthly or bi-monthly. Large bars and hotels, which have high sales and a lot of staff, often conduct a weekly stocktake. It is a common practice to employ an independent auditor to come each week to appraise the stock for the manager. The report will show if the bar has achieved its anticipated gross profit from the amount of stock sold. A weekly stocktake gives an excellent appraisal of how the business is performing, but it takes time and costs money.

Sales in January		$40,000
Opening stock	$10,000	
Food and beverage purchases	$15,000	
Less closing stock	$13,000	
Cost of goods sold (food and beverage)		$12,000
Gross Profit		**$28,000**
Gross Profit percentage		70%
Food (beverage) cost percentage		30%

Key Hospitality Operating Ratios. Like most businesses the hospitality industry use ratios to evaluate performance. The three most commonly used ratios are:

Food (beverage) Cost Percentage. This can be calculated weekly or monthly but is most valuable when calculated in conjunction with a stocktake.

$$\frac{\$ \text{ Cost of goods sold (purchases)}}{\$ \text{ Sales}}$$

See Chapter Five, *The Menu as a Management Tool* for more on this subject.

Gross Profit Percentage. This is the opposite of the food cost percentage

$$\frac{\$ \text{ Gross profit}}{\$ \text{ Sales}}$$

Labour Cost
$$\frac{\$ \text{ Cost of staff}}{\$ \text{ Sales}}$$

A business whose labour costs are over 38% will find it difficult to make money. Most restaurants would try to keep their wage cost to a maximum of 30–35% of sales.

Other important Ratios. In the hospitality industry it is possible to calculate ratios for each meal service (i.e. breakfast, lunch or dinner) per day, with totals for the week and for the month. Many restaurants wish to calculate the average spend of each diner (*cover*) during any meal service. They also may wish to calculate the revenue per seat as well as the staff to diner ratio.

Average spend per cover (per diner)	$\dfrac{\$ \text{ Total Sales for service}}{\$ \text{ Number of meals served in service}}$
Beverage sales compared to total sales	$\dfrac{\$ \text{ Total beverage sales}}{\$ \text{ Total sales}}$
Food sales compared to total sales	$\dfrac{\$ \text{ Total food sales}}{\$ \text{ Total sales}}$
Average spend per waiter	$\dfrac{\$ \text{ Total revenue for service}}{\$ \text{ Number of wait-staff per service}}$
Average spend for all staff	$\dfrac{\$ \text{ Total revenue for service}}{\$ \text{ Total number of staff per service}}$
Revenue per seat or per table	$\dfrac{\$ \text{ Revenue per period}}{\$ \text{ Number of seats (tables)}}$
Stock turn	$\dfrac{\$ \text{ Cost of goods sold}}{\$ \text{ Average stock held}}$
Net profit percentage	$\dfrac{\$ \text{ Net profit}}{\$ \text{ Sales}}$

Hospitality Industry Averages 1996[1]

Average food costs	37.96%
Labour/Wages cost	32.86%
Occupancy/rent	6.43%
Other operational costs	14.84%
Finance	1.26%
Depreciation	3.25%
Operating Profit	3.4%

FORECASTING SALES. The layout for the seating of the restaurant or café is critical to maximising your sales. The simple fact is that the more tables there are, the more customers can be seated and therefore the more you can sell. Having said that, it is better to have a small busy café than a large empty one. The use of *banquette* seating which lines the walls of a restaurant is a better use of space than having single chairs. Tables for two people are the most common seating request. In general, you can get more people seated at a round table than you can around a square but the latter is more versatile. It is easy to turn four square tables of two into a table for ten. Many cafés and restaurants will have a selection of different shaped tables for different uses.

As soon as you start pushing tables together, more space for additional tables becomes available. If you envisage catering for big groups at Christmas, it is always useful to have some spare tables and chairs. At Hay's, we have a seminar room adjacent to the restaurant that doubles as a private dining room. Even when the room is not in use, we constantly use its selection of chairs and tables as we cater for different numbers in the restaurant.

Calculating what you expect to sell on any one day is a difficult task. The best solution is to break down each day into the different meal services *(breakfast, morning tea, lunch, afternoon tea, dinner and supper)*. The next step is to estimate how many people will be served and what will be the average spend. Following this, it is possible to extrapolate these figures over the year.

Customer count: *But will you really get this number of customers?*

Week	Mon	Tue	Wed	Thu	Fri	Sat	Sun	Total Customers
Breakfast	20	20	20	20	20	30	0	130
Lunch	40	40	40	50	50	50	60	400
Dinner	20	20	30	30	50	50	*closed*	200

Average Spend: *But will they really spend this much?*		**Average Spend:** *Per Service*
Breakfast	130 x $6 = $780	$6 Croissant and coffee
Lunch	400 x $9.5 = $3800	$9.50 Panini, coffee and cake
Dinner	200 x $30 = $6000	$18 main, $7 dessert, $5 glass of wine

Total per week $10,580 X 52 weeks $550,160

It is important to remember that although there may be seating for 60, in reality, the maximum number will not be achieved during every service. Not every table of four will seat four people, it may only seat three people. If there is a big empty table, even a *"two"* will gravitate towards it, preferring its generous proportions to the cramped table for two in the corner. You may achieve a 70% occupancy during the lunch service but only 40% at night. Overestimating the occupancy may mean that it is difficult to achieve the sales forecast. Paying for that fabulous fit-out has just become more difficult!

FITTING OUT. For many, this is the moment they have been waiting for. However, being let loose with a cheque book may result in financial stress for many years. *Just remember the more you spend, the longer it will take to make* *a profit.* The *wish-list* for most people, must remain just that, as they temper their enthusiasm with prudence. You can always buy that spectacular painting later when you have some spare cash. It is important to reiterate that so often new businesses have a cash crisis during the start-up phase. *Do yourself a favour and leave some money in the bank, just for a rainy day.* It is a good idea to use a spreadsheet to help you analyse your set up. It is simple to *sum* and does not lie. It is also a simple task to delete things! Once the set-up costs are established then it is easier to work out a breakeven point for the venture.

If you are going to spend $100,000 on a fit-out, you need to achieve a minimum of $300,000–$400,000 in sales. The level of sales depends on the level of profit generated from each product sold. You need to be very clear on how you are going to generate this income. Remember that food and beverage sales will provide this income. This means that you must be very careful how to cost items on the menu.

Equipment. The equipment lists in the Appendix set out the sorts of equipment that you will need to set up a basic 50 seat restaurant and kitchen. Commercial kitchen equipment is expensive but it should last longer.

A caterer: from $10,000. This is the simplest form of set-up. A caterer often starts as an enthusiastic amateur at home. To grow the business however, Environmental Health Licences must be obtained from your Local Authority. To fit out a small kitchen with commercial grade appliances and no retail area will cost from $10,000.

A Café/Deli: $60,000. A simple set up with limited seating, a small basic kitchen and no bar would cost from $60,000.

A Bar: Basic bar $75,000 / Theme Bar $200,000. If a bar buys in most of its food and then re-heats it, the bar will need minimal cooking facilities. Theme bars which offer a comprehensive menu and therefore require a well-equipped kitchen are very expensive to set up.

A Restaurant: $150,000–$1.5 million. To create a destination where people wish to dine for an evening requires careful planing and expense. It will usually have a bar area and a well-equipped kitchen.

For a bar or restaurant, it is common to engage an architect or an interior designer to advise on the fit-out and design. It is good idea to use someone who has done this type of thing before and preferably with a list of previous fit-outs that you can check out. Quotes are essential. Cost over-runs are common so make sure that you have some cash reserves. It is always the expensive little things that get forgotten, such as the lighting or the dimmer system, the heat lamps or the outside speakers for the stereo.

To conclude this chapter, I suggest you consider the wise advice offered by Steven Brandt in his excellent book, *Entrepreneuring, The 10 Commandments for Building a Growth Company.*

BRANDT'S 10 COMMANDMENTS.[2]

1st Commandment: Limit the number of primary participants to people who can consciously agree upon and contribute directly to that which the enterprise is to accomplish, for whom, and by when.

2nd Commandment: Define the business of the enterprise in terms of what is to be bought, precisely by whom, and why.

3rd Commandment: Concentrate all available resources on accomplishing two or three specific operational objectives within a given time period.

4th Commandment: Prepare a written plan that delineates who in the total organisation is to do what, by when.

5th Commandment: Employ key people with proven records of success at doing what needs to be done in a manner consistent with the desired value system of the enterprise.

6th Commandment: Reward individual performance that exceeds agreed upon standards.

7th Commandment: Expand methodically from a profitable base toward a balanced business.

8th Commandment: Project, monitor and conserve cash and credit capability.

9th Commandment: Maintain a detached point of view.

10th Commandment: Anticipate incessant change.

---

1. Food Service Association of New Zealand, now called Restaurant Association of New Zealand 1996 Annual Survey compiled by Ross Melville PKF.

2. Brandt, S. *Entrepreneuring*, 1982.

CHAPTER FIVE

THE MENU AS A MANAGEMENT TOOL

Food and beverage are the products that we sell. Together they must provide sufficient income to pay for all the business expenses, service and repay the debts and give some return on the investment. Correct costing of these products is therefore the means by which the business will survive. This chapter explains the significance of the menu as a management tool.

The advent of the restaurant which was adopted first by France, has proved a boon to all citizens, and of great importance to the culinary art.

1. *By this means a man may dine at whatever hour suits him, according to the circumstances in which he is placed by his business or pleasure.*

2. *He can be sure of not going beyond the sum which he thinks fit to spend on his meal, for he knows the price of every dish before hand.*

Brillat-Savarin, The Physiology of Table.

WHAT SHOULD YOU CHARGE? A business must understand its cost structure and where it sits within the market. Understanding your competitors and their price structure will provide a clue for your pricing strategy. In the hospitality industry much depends on the experience that is being offered and the segments that are targeted. A takeaway in an industrial area will have a completely different cost structure to a café in the city centre. At a fine dining restaurant, customers will have certain expectations of the food quality, selection from the wine list, standard of service and price. These will be completely different from the expectations they have when eating lunch at their local café.

A *pricing strategy* determines the range of prices that can be charged for a product. You may sell muffins at $2, while the takeaway down the road sells a similar muffin for $1.50. How can you be sure that your muffins will sell at this price? If, as a special promotion, you then give away a muffin with every cup of coffee sold, what message does that send? This tells the customers that the muffin is not important. It is cheap to make and is therefore a cost-effective giveaway. When you want to start selling muffins again at $2, customers will say that you were happy to give them away in the past and $2 is too expensive.

Being busy and charging at a discount does not always work. Discounting does not necessarily result in increased profits. There is a cut-off point where the contribution margin has been so eroded by discounts that you would be better not offering a discount at all. It puts pressures on the gross profit and means that to meet the increased demand due to the discounts, you need to produce more food at the lower profit margin, employ more staff and buy more produce.

In the early 1990s, Bardellis, an innovator in the café-bar concept in Christchurch, offered pasta or pizza for two people priced at $12.50 on Monday and Tuesday nights. This was a very attractive offer and business was brisk on those nights. Over time however, they realised that in effect they were undermining everything else on their menu. The customers were not necessarily buying more beer or wine or dessert. They were busy but not profitable so a decision was made to drop the concept.

WHAT IS IN A PRICE. A price conveys a host of information. The price of a product or service can determine whether or not it is successful. Price must always be consistent with a customer's perception of value. The higher the price, the greater the consumer's expectation and the easier it is to disappoint. If a product is perceived to be too expensive, customers will find a substitute. If the product is priced too low, customers may feel that this reflects inferior quality.

Price Sensitivity. The economic phrase, **price elasticity of demand**, is a rather daunting way to express a customer's response and sensitivity to price. It measures how the quantity demanded of a product, changes in response to a change in the price. Price sensitivity *(price elasticity)* is demonstrated when an increase or decrease in the price produces an increase or decrease in demand.

When Bluff oysters first become available the price is high. At the beginning of the season, there will always be some consumers who want to buy the oysters irrespective of the price. They are said to be *price inelastic*. Other consumers, who feel that the price is too high may opt for the marine-farmed Pacific oysters *(a substitute)* because they are cheaper, and wait for the price of Bluff oysters to drop. These consumers demonstrate increased price elasticity in that they are more sensitive to price changes. By contrast consumers who are price inelastic will not change products on price. If the price goes up they will just pay the new price.

In the hospitality industry we can see this scenario working when people book accommodation. Many international tourists will not compromise on hotel facilities. The five-star ranking of hotels is an international system that consumers understand and when they book a hotel, they know the level of facilities and services offered. This is naturally reflected in the price. The price-sensitive traveller will shop around until they find the hotel with the right price. The price-insensitive traveller will just book and accept the price quoted. If all the hotels and motels are fully booked there are no substitutes for the price-sensitive traveller to choose from. They must take what is available and pay the market price. They are therefore a *price-taker* and are no longer price sensitive. *The greater the proportion of income spent on a good, that is, the more expensive the good, the greater the inelasticity.* People think more carefully about the purchase of a car than they do about buying a loaf of bread.

The greater the length of time following a price change, the higher the elasticity of demand. This is because, over time customers are able to develop substitutes and permanently change their buying patterns so that they may not return to the original product. To maintain market share and to remain competitive, the original product may be forced to meet the market by a drop in its price. During the 1990s there were several seasons when Bluff oysters were not harvested. Oyster lovers had to choose from Nelson oysters or Pacific oysters. Many people developed a preference for these oysters and when the Bluff oysters returned to the market, they were no longer interested in them or prepared to pay the premium price. The Nelson oysters and the Pacific oysters were a substitute and enabled consumers to alter their buying patterns.

Price Elasticity of Demand

This measures the responsiveness of quantity demanded of a good to a change in its price. It is affected by:

- The availability of substitutes.
- The proportion of income spent on the good. The more money spent, the greater the inelasticity. People think more carefully about the purchase of a car than they do about buying a loaf of bread.
- The amount of time elapsed since a price change. Over time customers are able to develop substitutes and permanently change their buying habits.

Pricing Strategies. Marketers talk about different pricing strategies. A *skimming strategy* is when the price is initially set high with the intention of reducing it when other competitors enter. We see this occurring in technology products such as cell phones, faxes and computers. A *penetration strategy* is when a new product is introduced at a low price to buy market share, deter competition and encourage people to try it. A *price leader* is when you set the price and this determines the price throughout the industry. A Steinlager stubbie could be an example of a price leader. Restaurants and bars throughout New Zealand charge a similar retail price for this product. Steinlager's main competitors are similarly priced. If the price of Steinlager went up, the chances are, its competitors would raise their prices to *meet the market. Price discrimination* is a strategy that caterers sometimes adopt. This is where they sell the same product at different prices. A caterer may evaluate what they consider the buyer's expectation of price, and price their product accordingly. The same analogy applies for hotel accommodation; if you do not ask about special discounts, you will not be offered them.

Predatory pricing is when prices are dropped to below cost in order to drive out competition or *beat the market*. During the 1990s, competition among pizza operators resulted in prices being forced down as more players entered the market. The so-called *pizza wars* have given consumers cheaper pizzas with free home delivery. Businesses like Pizza Hut have had to reposition themselves and move into a delivery and takeaway service, closing some of their unprofitable restaurants. In order to remain competitive Pizza Hut has had to meet the market on price and service.

Costing a Menu. There are many ways to cost a menu. One way is to look at the individual meal and cost each component separately. Alternatively, restaurants tend to cost out food in quantities that will serve 6, 12 or 20 covers. This works well if it is possible to accurately predict what will sell. What happens when you have costed a fish course on the expectation that you will sell 14 portions and in fact only sell 4? Does the costing reflect the fact that there will be some wastage? You may be able to sell the balance of the fish tomorrow night, but can you save the sauce or will it have to be thrown out?

GST. Believe it or not, it is common for people to forget that prices on invoices exclude GST ($12\frac{1}{2}$ percent). When the goods are delivered it is easy to glance at the price per product and forget about the GST component at the bottom of the invoice. The consequences are obvious. You have unintentionally discounted your product and what is more you will not achieve the desired gross profit. Once the food costs have been calculated, then GST must be added on.

Costing formulae. There are many variables that play havoc with the food costings. In Chapter Four, we discussed some accounting terms and ratios that enable a business to determine how it is going. The cost of goods sold figure indicates the cost of the food and beverage sold. This figure will show whether you have achieved the desired food cost ratio. So often a business costs food at 33% of the retail price to find that when the actual results are finalised by the accountant, they in fact show 38%. This is the most common problem in the hospitality industry. If the food cost is now 38%, you have just lost 5% off the bottom line.

Price-led costing. This is when you cost a product on what you believe the customer is prepared to pay. The *educated guess*, otherwise called the *back of a matchbox method*, is when the ingredients are jotted down roughly on a piece of paper using approximate prices and quantities. The price is then determined by the cost of the ingredients and the expectation of what the market will pay. There is no consistency between the retail price of one product and another so there is no certainty that the gross profit will be achieved. Costing this way can be just an intuitive guess. This is a risky approach for a business that wants to achieve long term growth and profitability.

In New Zealand, the common method of costing is called the **food cost percentage** or **cost-led pricing**. This takes the cost of the food and adds on a mark-up (ratio) to give a retail price. This method of costing calculates the same mark-up for all the dishes on a menu. It does not reflect the direct labour that it takes to make each product. Some products require a lot of preparation and others very little. Costing this way can make a restaurant uncompetitive in what it charges. Just picking a food-cost percentage of say 33%, without consideration of your fixed costs, is not meaningful. A food cost percentage of 28% may be more appropriate.

The **contribution margin costing method** is commonly used in North America and evaluates the individual products in terms of what they contribute to gross profit *(contribution margin)*. This method was originally devised by Kasavana and Smith[1] and is referred to as *menu engineering*. The focus is on the gross profit generated per product. To remain competitive in a large market you must meet the market on price. This may mean that if sirloin steak is the most popular meal and each night you sell 100 portions, then you have the volume to justify a reduction in prices. The cost of preparing an additional steak meal is far less than it is to prepare the other meals. To compete on price with other restaurants you are able to *discount* or *price cut* and drop the price charged. Once you know the gross profit achieved from a product it is easy to discount with confidence. This method analyses each product on the gross profit it achieves and then ranks the product.

The Boston Consulting Group, a respected firm of American business consultants, came up with the concept known as the *growth/share analysis*.[2] This is used to evaluate different products offered by a business in terms of their market growth rate and the relative market share. This idea has become common parlance today, when products get referred to as *dogs* or *cash cows*. The concept has been translated into one relevant to the hospitality industry where the menu is evaluated for popularity and gross profit contribution. *Stars or primes*[3] are products with high sales and low food costs. These are the most desirable products. A *cash cow* or *plow horse* is a product with high sales but a low contribution margin. It may be a product that lures the customer through the door, like a bottle of milk or plate of french fries. A *problem child* or *puzzle* is a product that has potential and could turn into a star or a dog. It may be a dish on the menu that has a high contribution margin but low sales such as a vegetarian main course. A *dog* offers no benefit with low sales and low profit margin and should be abandoned.

Best Method. Any costing formula is individual to the business. The most effective costing is an amalgamation of all of the methods mentioned above and summarised in the following box.

1. Calculate your fixed costs to determine the break-even point.
2. Determine a food cost percentage that fits your business.
3. Assess your individual products for their contribution margin.
4. Evaluate your competition.
5. Meet the market and price according to your market's perception of value.

Determining Fixed Costs. The first step is to determine the fixed costs that the business must meet each week and each month. If the business is located in a small suburban shopping centre, its rental will be substantially less than if it is located in a prime retail area. If the business has had an inexpensive fit-out then the break-even point will be lower than with an expensive fit-out. The first costs to determine are the rent, depreciation on fixed assets, interest on term loans, insurance, power (gas, electricity), telephone/communication charges and basic administration. In addition it is important to add the salaries or wages of key employees without whom the business could not operate. The smaller the business, the fewer people would fit into this category. At a minimum it would include the chef/cook and manager.

Accountants tend to treat the owner's financial return as whatever money is left once all the expenses have been paid. As an owner, it is important to calculate the cost of your input into the business, especially if you are a key staff member. The opportunity cost for *you* needs to be considered. *What else could you be doing with your time?* You could have another job that constitutes a better use of your time rather than making cappuccinos which you can pay someone $10 per hour to do. If you have invested money in the business, it is important to consider the opportunity cost of that money. There must be a return on that investment and the capital employed. Would investing the money at a bank offer a better return? To say that *"It's my money and I don't care about the return"* is deluding yourself. There must be some benefit and justification for the investment.

If you have $100,000 invested in the fixed assets and working capital, an average return on the investment for a hospitality business would be 8-10%. To borrow this money from a bank you would have to pay a similar amount in interest depending on the interest rates at the time. Banks would also require principal repayments.

Approximate fixed costs (excl GST)

Interest on an investment of $100,000	$10,000
Rent, rates, operating expenses	$40,000
Depreciation	$10,000
Insurance	$2,500
Power: Gas/electricity	$6,000
Telephone	$1,500
Administration	$5,000
Manager (yourself?)	$35,000
Chef	$30,000
	$140,000

Divide the total fixed costs by
the number of days open
6 days per week x 52 weeks =312 days.......... **$449** per day ex GST
for a 30-seat café .... **$14.97** per seat per day ex GST

The following table illustrates a 30-seat café, open only during the day, six days per week, with the above fixed costs. It achieves average sales per seat of $32; of this $11 goes in food, $15 in fixed costs and $6 for all other expenses including profit. If the café decided to open for the evening trade, these figures would change and the sales per seat would increase, but so would the overheads.

30 seat café open for 6 days per week (no nights) excl GST

		per year	per week	seats per year	per seat per day
Sales		$300,000	$5,769	9360	$32
Food costs	33%	$100,000	$1,923	9360	$11
Fixed costs	47%	$140,000	$2,692	9360	$15
Other costs and profit	20%	$60,000	$1,154	9360	$6
	100%				

Food Cost Percentage. The following table sets out some common costing percentages and how to calculate them. This is just a guide and there is nothing to stop you from using a food cost percentage of 31% or 29% depending on your cost structure. As we have previously discussed, the lower the food cost, the higher the gross profit and the more money available to pay the bills. The only way to obtain a true gross profit is to conduct regular stocktakes. Many large organisations will do this weekly, particularly for beverages. It provides a regular check that the gross profit has been achieved and will also alert the management to any incidences of theft. To conduct a weekly stocktake, there needs to be appropriate resources to process it. If it takes three or four weeks just to do the administration then it is a waste of time. Some organisations employ consultants who specialise in doing stocktakes on their behalf.

To price a menu with a food cost of 25%
Multiply the ingredient cost by 4 and this will give you a Gross
  Profit of 75%.
This would apply to restaurants and bars, including those in
  hotels, with high set-up costs.

To price a menu with a food cost of 33%.
Multiply the ingredient cost by 3 and this will give you a Gross
  Profit of 67%. This would apply to the majority of restaurants,
  cafés and bars.

To price a menu with a food cost of 40%
Multiply the ingredient cost by 2.5 and this will give you a Gross
  Profit of 60%. This would apply to simple food outlets with low
  set up costs, such as tea rooms and takeaway businesses.

Not all food and beverage purchases are turned into a product consumed by the customers. There are many ways in which the food cost percentage that is used to calculate the price is affected. *Yield* is one of the underlying principles of costing. It is important to determine how many portions a recipe will yield. In doing so you are able to more accurately estimate the cost per portion and therefore the gross profit. Every time a staff member helps themselves to a slice of that delicious smoked salmon, the cost of using that product changes.

Poor costing of menus affects profitability

1. **GST on invoices.** Remember that prices on invoices exclude GST (12½%). Once the food costs have been calculated, GST must be added.

2. **Seasonal price fluctuations.** Be aware of price changes. For example, in winter the price of tomatoes can double overnight.

3. **Yield per dish.** Problems can occur when buying 2 kilograms of fillet steak and expecting to get 10 x 200 gram portions but in fact getting only 7 mixed grade portions.

4. **Poor portion control.** This is caused by a lack of standard measures (e.g. ladles, cups, ramekins) or being too generous with the portions.

5. **Bad menu planning.** This can be a case of too many dishes and/or too many ingredients.

6. **Spoilage.** This can result from not taking care of ingredients (bruising, food left un-refrigerated, etc).

7. **Wastage.** Food may be thrown out because it has spoiled or you have over-catered.

8. **Inaccurate ordering of supplies.** Over-ordering of perishable products results in a surplus which must be used up.

9. **Inaccurate forecasting of demand.** If too much food is prepared it will have to be thrown out.

10. **Lack of standardised recipes with an expected yield.** Each time a dish is made, it turns out differently with variable yields.

11. **Human error.** The recipe is not followed correctly, for example, forgetting to add the baking powder to a muffin mix.

12. **Faulty equipment results in spoilage.** A food processor with a blunt blade fails to purée the vegetables so they have to be sieved by hand.

13. **Poor security.** Produce is stolen by customers or staff.

14. **Staff meals.** Often the impact on the food costs of feeding 10 staff two meals 7 days per week is not appreciated.

15. **Taking food/beverages for your own use.** Remember that every time you help yourself to another glass of wine, it is affecting the cost of goods sold.

The table below illustrates that if you have a food cost of $2 then the retail price, if working on a food cost percentage of 33%, should be $6.75. Conversely if you see on a menu a price of $16.95 for a chicken breast then that should denote a food cost of approximately $5. I know that does sound scary but remember all those other costs!

Standard Costing Formula. Cost of ingredients x 3 (food cost of 33%) x 1.125 (GST) = retail price

Food cost	Food cost 33%	GST	Retail price
$2.00	$6.00	$0.75	$6.75
$3.00	$9.00	$1.25	$10.12
$4.00	$12.00	$1.50	$13.50
$5.00	$15.00	$1.87	$16.87

A spreadsheet is by far the best method to use when calculating food costs. While there are software packages available that offer a food costing programme, a spreadsheet is cheap and flexible. Costing a menu does take time especially if you have not done it before. But knowledge is power and you will be surprised at how products cost out. In the Appendix there is a costing example for you to try.

OTHER MENU CONSIDERATIONS. When the Christmas season comes around and there is pressure to take large groups, do not hesitate to offer a set menu at a fixed price. A choice of two entreés and two or three main courses followed by two desserts is quite acceptable. This is actually a *win-win*. The diners know how much the meal will cost plus they may get a better deal, for example, three courses for $35 rather than the usual price of $40. The café now has a better idea of what to prepare and with a smaller choice, the kitchen will be able to cook the meal faster. Large groups can be a mixed blessing. While they fill the restaurant, they will often take over as their exuberance escalates, upsetting the quieter tables.

Buying in Products. It is often difficult to assess the costs and benefits of using convenience products that are bought in. If a business requires large quantities of pastry, it is far more cost effective to buy it in. If the restaurant wishes to bake a *tart au citron* for the dessert menu, the competitive advantage may lie in the fact that it makes its own pastry. If the business is a café or tearooms, the cost of buying in cakes and sandwiches can be prohibitive. This can destroy the food cost percentage and, on top of this, the staff lose the skills and initiative to bake themselves. The core competencies of the food business may be undermined.

The Experience Curve. The more you cook, the more efficient you get. Business consultants talk of the *experience curve* which is a concept demonstrating that people learn through repetition and experience. As the staff accumulate experience and understand the task, the costs of making a product should decrease. In a menu we see evidence of this in that when a menu is first changed it can take some time to get used to the new products. Once the menu has been cooked a few times, the chefs get more experienced at cooking it and become efficient.

STEPS TO ACHIEVE MAXIMUM COST EFFICIENCY
- standardise recipes with standard yields
- standardise portion size
- utilise staff time efficiently
- utilise equipment productively

1. Kasavana, M. and Smith, D. *Menu Engineering – A practical guide to Menu Analysis*, 1982.
2. Assael, *Marketing Principles and Strategy*, 1993.
3. Pavesic, D. in *Fundamental Principles of Restaurant Control 1998* uses the terms Primes, Standard, Sleepers and Problems. Coltman, M. in *Hospitality Management Accounting* 1998 uses the terms Stars, Plow horses, Puzzles and Dogs.

CHAPTER SIX

CONSTRUCTING A MENU

The menu is the key marketing tool for a café or restaurant. It projects the personality of the place and communicates a message to the diners and prospective diners. The menu must embody the vision and therefore be consistent with the goals of the business. This chapter explores the issues involved in constructing a menu and wine list, as well as suggests guidelines for matching food with wine.

We eat with our eyes. The food we like to eat in cafés and restaurants is not the same that we cook at home. It should be different, perhaps introducing a new ingredient or new combinations of ingredients. There should always be an element of surprise in a dish. How the food is presented is also part of the experience. A quiche slapped on a plate and reheated in the microwave will not evoke the same response as a freshly baked quiche, still warm from the oven, served with a small *mesclun* salad and *vinaigrette*. To use Tom Peters' phrase again,[1] we are in the *"Pursuit of WOW!"* The goal in constructing a menu is how to *WOW* the customers with a menu that reads well, tastes great and makes them smile while achieving the sales and profit goals of the business.

The vigor of seasonal, fresh, raw food in their prime is a powerful incentive to a cook whose imagination is not limited by the strictures of a fixed repeated menu.

A menu that does not excite those who cook it, will not excite those who eat it.

A menu that reflects a cook's joy and whimsy makes the table an abiding source of pleasure.

Paul Bertolli,
in **Chez Panisse Cooking**

Menu types. Menus can take a variety of formats. The *à la carte* menu is set out on card or paper *(carte)* and the diner chooses what to eat from a selection of appetisers, entrées, main courses and desserts. Currently this would be the most common form of menu in New Zealand. A *blackboard* menu will change regularly and is often used in conjunction with an *à la carte* menu to describe the day's specials. A *static* menu is one that does not change. McDonald's menu would be an example of this. *Cycle* menus are used by the airlines with the selection of menus rotating in weekly cycles. The *table d'hôte* is a set menu with little choice at a fixed price *(prix fixe)*. This is the traditional menu of the French bistro. Restaurants like Chez Panisse[2] near San Francisco offer this style of menu. The menu is determined each week and has a different price structure depending on the night of the week. Some restaurants in New Zealand offer a *menu dégustation* which is a 5–8 course tasting menu of small courses. Each course is often matched with wine.

The Menu layout. David Pavesic[3] in his book, *Fundamental Principles of Restaurant Cost Controls*, emphasises the fact that, in general, a customer takes *109 seconds* to read a menu. The layout of the menu and wine list will affect which items sell best. People recall the first or last thing that they saw on the menu so a menu should not be a confusing jumble of words. If prices are placed in a column, it is natural for the eye to skim down this rather than take in each line of description. In other words, if you want people to buy on price, then put the prices in a column. To avoid this, place the prices at then end of the line and use a smaller font size.

Tarakihi with fresh apricot and coriander salsa	$20
Sirloin with rösti potatoes and anchovy butter	$22
Rack of lamb with fresh mint and roast garlic jus	$26

Tarakihi with fresh apricot and coriander salsa $20

Sirloin with rösti potatoes and anchovy butter $22

Rack of lamb with fresh mint and roast garlic jus $26

The paper or card on which the menu is printed has an impact on how the customer views the restaurant. The colour and texture of the paper, the size, the font used and its size are important considerations. The words used to describe the dishes on the menu must attempt to paint a picture and to make the diner salivate in anticipation. Avoid verbose descriptions that list every ingredient. They can be very tedious to read and also set the restaurant up for criticism. ... *"On the menu, it said salmon with vanilla infusion, chervil, tamari and lemon. Where was the tamari?"* Only a drop of tamari may have been used.

WHAT TO PUT ON THE MENU. A well-balanced menu should appeal to a cross-section of diners and should be able to help the diner select the choice that they feel like eating. *"What do I feel like to eating tonight? Do I feel like fish or steak? Do I feel like something deep-fried and crunchy or a healthy salad?"* The menu must then offer a choice to meet this need without falling into the trap of repeating the techniques or the commodities.

Unless the business is a specialist vegetarian café, most customers would expect to see one of the following proteins, either as an entrée or main course:

- beef (sirloin, T-bone, rump)
- lamb (rack, fillets, rump)
- chicken (thighs, breast, drums)
- pork fillet
- fish, shell fish
- a vegetarian dish

Other specialist products that are popular are Cervena (NZ farm-raised venison), duck, pheasant, ostrich and offal. If the clientèle is not price-sensitive then it is easy to include products like extra virgin olive oil, saffron, paua and truffles. Nelson scallops, a New Zealand delicacy, often wholesales at nearly $40 per kilo and is therefore too expensive for most restaurants.

At Hay's we always struggle with the vegetarian course. In one week, we may sell only one meal. We offer a vegetarian course to give our customers a choice, but we must ensure that it is able to be cooked to our standard during the dinner service. It must not be too complicated or time consuming. Since the dish is made irregularly, it always takes longer to cook and causes far more stress during the dinner service than all the other meals!

Paul Bertolli,[4] a former head chef at Chez Panisse, describes a successful menu as *"... a harmony of parts and a succession of individual dishes, each of which declares a mood, weight and style".*

A good menu provides contrast because variety in cooking styles and ingredients keeps the consumer's interest. Within a dish there should be a variety of textures to satisfy the palate. If every ingredient is soft to eat, it does not challenge the palate. Use of colour provides impact and a natural garnish. If everything is brown or deep-fried, it is not so pleasing to the eye. *Fresh and seasonal* is the catch-cry of the chef. Seasonal ingredients are also plentiful and therefore cheaper to put on the menu.

Seasonality. In recent times, many products have become available throughout the year as people seek to meet the demand and product is sourced from overseas. The consequence of this is that when the New Zealand season arrives, the WOW is lost. Strawberries, basil, and *new* potatoes have all somehow lost that *specialness*. Frozen and tinned products have also cheapened the fresh product. Think of all those delicious fresh pineapples wilting on supermarket shelves because the novelty has been destroyed by the tinned version. Similarly, few restaurants would put peas on a menu because the frozen product has commoditised the pea experience. Fresh corn is sensational, but its *specialness* has been undermined by the frozen and canned product.

Nutrition. A dish on a menu should be nutritionally balanced. It is important to think in terms of the different food groups. The protein is usually the *hero* of the dish, and the vegetables are the accompaniment, while the carbohydrate is the *filler*. A meal should make the diner feel replete and to do this most effectively, each course must have some type of starch (bread, rice, pasta, potatoes, etc). How many times have you asked for bread to mop up that delicious sauce languishing on your plate?

Getting to WOW. To create a memorable eating experience, the most effective way is to pick one or two ingredients in each dish and make a statement out of them. *Less is more.* Creating a hero of the dish and focusing just on that product will help you achieve a WOW. Repetition of ingredients destroys the *specialness*. Basil used in the entrée should not be used again in the main course. Repetition of cooking styles destroys the impact and may make the diner feel that the chef's skills are limited.

> **Simple menu descriptions that focus on the hero of the dish**
>
> New season's *Asparagus* with lemon and chive butter
> *Field Mushrooms* with sherry cream
> *Wild Duck* with tangerine glaze
> *Organic vine-ripened tomatoes* with fresh tarragon and *Balsamico*

The cleaner and more obvious the taste, the easier it is for the diner to appreciate. *"Yes, the asparagus were delicious. The lemon really brought out the flavour"*. Too many ingredients confuse the palate and leave no one satisfied. Having said that, it is always exciting to introduce a new flavour, hidden in one of the accompaniments. Freshly grated nutmeg sprinkled on potatoes, lime juice squeezed over resting chicken breasts, hidden sprigs of herbs incorporated in a *mesclun* salad.

Desserts. On an *à la carte* menu, one would expect to see a small selection of well-chosen desserts. This would usually include an ice cream, something with chocolate *(a chocolate WOW)*, something fruity, something baked and perhaps gooey and a cheese course. For the diner, the choice of dessert will often be determined by the previous courses. Eating three courses full of cream is exhausting so a light and fruity dessert is appropriate. A fruit *sorbet* can be an excellent way to finish a meal. Depending on the size and competency of the kitchen, cooking desserts to order may not be advisable. It can put enormous pressure on the kitchen during a busy dinner service especially when oven space is at a premium. When Peter Thornley was at French Farm, he would cook an incredible caramel soufflé to order, but the waiting staff would inform the customer of the 25-minute delay.

THE MENU

Hors d'oeuvres (optional). Allow 2–3 savouries per person before a dinner. In doing this course you may avoid having an entrée.

Appetiser/Entrée. This should be light, appetising and provocative. This is not the main course and therefore should be small and not too filling.

Sorbet. This is a palate cleanser that adds interest.

Dinner. Meat and fish fillets: 180–250g average portion size
        One chicken breast: 160–200g
        Sauce: 30–50ml per person
        Vegetables: a selection of two or three

Dessert. This should make everyone feel good; replete.
A heavy or spicy main course should be followed by a light fruity dessert.

Cheese. In France, cheese will be served before dinner. Cheese can be superfluous to a well-balanced meal but may be a substitute for dessert.

Petits fours/friandise. Rather than a big dessert why not offer delicious truffles or pastries with coffee?

WINE LISTS. It goes without saying that if you want to sell wines effectively, you must have staff who are knowledgeable and can advise the diners on their choice of wine. The style of the business will again affect the size of a wine list. A small well-chosen wine list can satisfy discerning customers just as well as the 400-bottle wine list. With over 300 New Zealand wineries to choose from, plus many more imported wines, there is an enormous selection available. Given such a choice, it is always disappointing to see whole wine lists constructed around one or two companies.

Constructing wine lists
1. Organise the wine list into a structure with a font size that is easy to read.
2. List the main wine varietals.
3. Ensure a selection of wines from different wineries with a choice of price range.
4. Always offer a selection of wines by the glass with a range of prices. It is a good idea to offer quality wines at a more expensive price as well as cheaper wine.
5. Make sure you have the wine in stock.
6. List the vintage and tell the customers if it has changed. There can be considerable variation from one vintage to the next.

The most effective layout is when the wine list is broken down into categories. The most common categories are by wine varietal (wine variety). A varietal group can then be broken down in a number of ways, for instance:
- lowest price → highest price
- highest price → lowest price
- lighter style → full bodied style

A restaurant with an extensive wine list of imported wines may choose to list them under the country of origin. *Terroir* is a term used to describe the distinctive style of a wine growing area which is influenced by climate, soil, landscape and even culture. As the different *terroir* of New Zealand emerge, a wine list can also be organised by region.

At Hay's we use a simple categorisation that enables the diner to scan for the varietal, vintage, winery name, region and price. While there has been a trend to include on a wine list tasting notes and food matching suggestions, we find it is better to let our staff discuss the wine match with the customer and make appropriate recommendations.

Grape variety: Cabernet Sauvignon				
Vintage	Name	Region	Price per bottle	Price per glass
1998	Te Mata	Hawkes Bay	$35	$7.50

On a wine list the varietals should appear in the order that they would be consumed. It is common to see Champagne and Méthodes at the beginning of the list while dessert wines and ports come at the end. The composition of the wine list should also reflect the seasons. During the summer, chilled white wine tends to be more popular than in the middle of winter. To reflect this, a wine list may offer a bigger selection of white wines in the summer than it does in the winter.

Varietals should appear in the following order on a wine list
1. **Champagne.** Only sparkling wine produced in the region of Champagne should be listed here.
2. **Méthode Traditionelle.** Wine made in a Champagne-style.
3. **White Wine.**
   - Lighter bodied aromatic white wines: Riesling, Sauvignon Blanc, Chenin Blanc, Pinot Gris, Muller Thurgau, Gerwurztraminer, Semillon.
   - Full bodied white wine: Chardonnay, some Gerwurztraminer.
4. **Red Wines.**
   - Lighter bodied red wines: Rosé, Pinot Noir, Beaujolais, Grenache.
   - Full bodied red wines: Cabernet Sauvignon, Merlot, Shiraz.
5. **Dessert Wines.**
6. **Ports or muscats.** An authentic Port from Portugal, Muscat from Rutherglen.

Changing a wine list. It seems that as soon as you update a wine list and print it on a quality paper something changes. It may be the vintage or perhaps a wine has become unavailable. Around September–October each year, there are many new releases with trade shows and promotions to attend. I always try to wait until after I have attended these shows and tasted the new releases before changing the wine list at Hay's. For us, this is the main time to change the wine list. During the rest of the year we just tinker with the basic list. While the larger wine companies offer the service of printing a wine list, it is contingent on the number of their wines that you place. For a new business, there are many advantages in taking up the offer of these companies because it can save you money. They may also offer staff training and promotional support such as aprons, umbrellas, T-shirts and flyers.

Bring Your Own. *Bring your own wine* harks back to the days when there were only a few licensed restaurants. Diners would turn up at a restaurant with anything from a cask of wine to a keg of beer. Changes to drink-driving offences and the host responsibility of licensees mean that the *laissez faire* approach of the past is no longer acceptable. Customers will hunt out BYO restaurants because of the saving in the cost of wine. At Hay's we still offer the BYO option although I am ambivalent about this. BYO people tend to drink more and then argue over their bill and especially the corkage charge. Sometime I take time to explain to people why there is a charge. It is the substitution effect. If they did not bring wine then the diners would have to buy something off the wine list. The opportunity cost for a restaurant offering BYO is considerable. It is a sale lost. However, it is also a sale gained in that these customers are dining with you rather than anybody else! This still remains an attractive market segment to target.

In New Zealand you will pay between $3 and $10 per bottle for corkage. At Chez Panisse they charge $US15 plus tax for the privilege. Even by charging $5 per bottle, the restaurant does not recover the costs to service the wine. Cleaning of the wine glasses after each service and the cost to replace breakages all mount up. I once served a woman who disappeared after I had gone through the wine list and made a wine recommendation. A while later she returned with the exact bottle I had suggested. The woman had gone back to her car, rushed down to a liquor store and taken my advice. I was somewhat incredulous when she gave me the bottle to open!

COSTING BEVERAGES. Just like your menu, what you charge for your beverages will also have a direct impact on the financial viability of the business. The house wines are usually the wines that businesses expect to sell the most of and therefore should be the wines with the best margins. The average retail mark-up on wines is anywhere between 80%–150%. Older vintages, particularly gold medal winners may be more expensive because of the holding time to allow them to age. Quality hotels and restaurants often charge more to reflect their overheads. Wines by the glass will always be slightly more expensive than the full bottle price. This reflects the additional cost that is incurred by offering wine by the glass. Every bar owner in New Zealand will tell you how difficult it is to pour the standard five 150ml glasses from a 750ml bottle of wine. It seems that another bottle always needs to be opened to get the final 100ml of wine. In doing this, the anticipated yield has not been achieved, plus another bottle has been opened which must now be sold before it oxidises and spoils.

When costing beverages, it is often more appropriate to use a contribution margin evaluation to help determine the prices to charge. Beverages are more price sensitive than a lot of food products. For example a business would have difficulty pricing a well-known wine such as Lindauer at too high a level, when consumers know that they can purchase it for under $10 at the supermarket.

The table below shows the different retail margins that can be charged and their contribution to gross profit. Canned or bottled drinks can be the lowest performers of all. This explains why many hospitality businesses install a Post-mix system for non-alcoholic beverages and prefer to sell tap beer rather than stubbies. A bar makes more money on mixing a vodka, lime and lemonade than it does from selling the fashionable Ready to drink (RTD) mixes.

AVERAGE SALES PER WEEK

Qty Sold	Beverages	Cost	Retail margin	Sales excl GST	Sales incl GST	Contri- bution	Sales ex GST	Contri- bution to GP	% of sales
120	Cola	$1.25	128%	$1.60	$1.80	$0.35	$192.00	$42.00	8%
150	Beer Stubbies	$1.28	278%	$3.56	$4.00	$2.28	$533.33	$341.33	21%
30	Sparkling	$8.90	220%	$19.56	$22.00	$10.66	$586.67	$319.67	23%
24	Shiraz	$13.50	184%	$24.89	$28.00	$11.39	$597.33	$273.33	24%
15	Chardonnay	$20.00	200%	$40.00	$45.00	$20.00	$600.00	$300.00	24%
						Total sales	$2,776.00		

In the example above the cola that sells for $1.80 will contribute 35 cents profit per bottle. The shiraz that costs $13.50 to buy, will retail at $28 including GST and of this, the business will make $11.39 per bottle. The $20 bottle of chardonnay, with a standard 100% mark up will retail at $45 including GST and the business will make $20 per bottle. The chardonnay may be three years old and no longer available through liquor outlets. To have it in stock, the restaurant may have bought three cases two years ago. The retail margin should reflect the holding time for that product.

Just as we discussed when costing a menu, once the business understands its margins and where the profit comes from, it is able to discount on quantity. In the table above, it would be a mistake to offer a cola at a discount, but the business could run a chardonnay promotion at a lesser price.

MATCHING FOOD WITH WINE. Much has been made in recent years of the secrets of matching food with wine. There is really no mystery and it is quite a simple task. The most important aspect in determining a good match, is to understand the varietal characteristics of the wine. These are the flavours that the wine imparts both as a smell and when tasting. The *aroma* is the varietal characteristics that the grape displays. It you picked a sauvignon blanc grape from the vine, you would recognise some of the flavours that appear in the wine. The *bouquet* is the smell of the wine but includes the influences of the winemaking process. Use of oak barrels for fermentation or ageing may be evident in the bouquet. With food, the key to wine matching is to replicate the flavours of the wine in the dish. A chardonnay may be described as *ripe tropical fruit, citrus with a hint of oak*. This could be matched with a roasted chicken breast with lemon (citrus) and a pawpaw (tropical fruit) salsa.

Understanding your palate. Tasting wine without food is a completely different experience from tasting wine with food. Your palate changes. The first step is to understand how we taste.

- Sweetness is sensed on the tip of the tongue and is a fleeting sensation which is one of the reasons why we want to take a second mouthful.
- Acidity (sourness) is tasted on the sides of the tongue.
- Flavour and saltiness is tasted down the middle of the tongue.
- Bitterness lingers at the back of the tongue and is often not apparent until the food has been swallowed (think of grapefruit).

For food or wine to have a well-developed and full-bodied taste, it is important to have a little of all of these things, excluding bitterness. Sugar or honey will bring the flavour forward on the tongue. You will taste this first. Acid (lemon juice, vinegar, wine) gives complexity, crispness and freshness. Salt and pepper add flavour. Fat coats your mouth and that is why it feels so good. It is smooth and creamy.

When we taste wines, we experience the same sensations. Ripe fruit in wine gives the initial sweetness we crave. Acidity gives life to the wine. If there was no acid, the wine would taste like cordial with alcohol. In red wine we taste tannins which give the chewy, dry feel in the mouth and a lingering finish.

When matching food with wine it is important to consider how sweet the wine or the food will be. A sweet meal will taste sweeter if paired with a dry wine, at the same time the wine will taste dryer and more acidic. A full bodied wine can overpower the more subtle flavours of the food. The ripe oaky chardonnay that we so like to drink, is often too flavoursome for the food it is paired with. The herbaceous sauvignon blanc, that first drew international attention to New Zealand wines, can be so fresh and fruity that it is difficult to match with delicately flavoured food. I prefer to serve it as an *apéritif*. With red wine, the deliciously fruity shiraz with it velvet mouth feel is a great match for strong flavoured foods but it too can overpower and confuse the palate. When matching a menu with wines it is important not to overwork the palate so that the following course is deflated and empty because you have lost all sensitivity to taste.

Change the wine. Gone are the days when we drank the same wine from the beginning to the end of a meal. Did you ever wonder why that delicious dessert that you laboured over tasted so ordinary when it came time to eat it? It was probably because you still had half a glass of cabernet to finish. Changing wine as you change the course makes a menu so much more interesting. This alone can be a *WOW*. The change complements the menu and helps the diner to focus on the different tastes that the meal and the wines create.

Beyond understanding the flavours of the wine, there are certain generally accepted rules.[5] How you follow these rules depends on your confidence with the wine match. If you know it works well but involves an unusual combination, just do it!

1. **White wine with white meat and fish; red wines with red meat.** If in doubt follow this rule. If however you are serving chicken with a heavy red wine sauce, then it is appropriate to use a red wine to match.

2. **Replicate the flavours of the wine in the food.** It is often easier to choose the wine first and build a menu to match.

3. **Start with the lightest wines working to the most full-bodied.**
   - Méthode traditonelle → canapés
   - Chardonnay → monk fish with vanilla beurre blanc
   - Merlot → fillet steak with mustard and red-wine jus
   - Noble Riesling → rata honey crème brûlée

4. **Food with a lot of fat** should be matched with a dry wine with good acidity.

5. **Delicate food** should be matched with delicate wines.

6. **Richly flavoured food** should be matched with full-bodied wines.

7. **White wines and Méthodes should be served chilled.** In winter it is important not to over chill the wines and often room temperature will be quite acceptable.

8. **Decant red wines.** Young full-bodied tannic wines are greatly helped by decanting into a jug. The wine can then be poured back into a bottle. This process can oxidise the wine sufficiently to open up the flavours.

9. **Méthode traditonelle.** This style of wine makes an excellent alternative to a dessert wine or port. It can provide a satisfactory match for a chocolate dessert. Serving *bubbles* at the conclusion to a meal will facilitate the party!

10. **Have a beer.** For food with a lot of chillies and spice it better to enjoy the taste sensation and forget about a wine. Wine with spicy food compromises the quality of the wine. Chilli alters the sensitivity of your palate.

Wine temperature. The colder the wine, the faster you will drink it. It dulls the taste buds. Consumers will drink more if the wine is chilled. Think of how you react to a warm beer, the flavour is so much stronger that is difficult to quench a thirst. This is the same for wine. Unchilled wine tastes completely different from the chilled option. Do not be afraid to serve white wine, like chardonnay or riesling, at a warmer temperature because you will taste far more of the wine's flavours.

Recommended temperatures

Dessert and sparking wines	4–8°C
White wines	8–12°C
Red wines and Port	18–20°C

Decanting. As red wine ages, sediment starts to settle in the bottom of the bottle. When serving red wine, decanting into a jug will achieve two things. Firstly the sediment will be poured off and secondly, the oxidation that happens during decanting will open the wine so that the flavours will be more apparent. Uncorking a bottle only serves to oxidise the small portion of the neck that is open to the air. Young full-bodied tannic wines are greatly helped by decanting.

1. Peters, T. *The Pursuit of WOW!* 1994.
2. You can view the weekly menu of Chez Panisse on their website http://www.chezpanisse.com.
3. Pavesic, D. *Fundamental Principles of Restaurant Cost Control*, 1998.
4. Paul Bertolli with Alice Waters *Chez Panisse Cooking*, 1988.
5. Hospitality Standards Institute, *Certificate in Wine Handbook*.

CHAPTER SEVEN

BUILDING A TEAM

W hether you are the owner of the business or its manager, you are in a leadership role. This chapter looks at the characteristics of leaders and the skills that help them in their tasks.

LEADERSHIP. To be a leader you must be able to build a motivated team of people who identify with what you are trying to achieve. I personally struggle with the leadership classification, but at my work, everyone knows that I am the person where the *buck stops*, the person with the vision and the strategy, *whether I like it or not.* Tom Peters calls a leader, the *chief dispenser of enthusiasm*[1].

Good leaders are good teachers in the sense that they liberate the creative energies of others. A leader is akin to a conductor. While each instrument in the orchestra is valued and individual, the conductor pulls them together to create harmonies and timbre that would never be apparent otherwise. Just as the conductor's plans for the orchestra can be undermined, so too can the leader's plans be sabotaged by uncooperative staff.

In a hospitality business, there can be a number of leaders. The owner, who may or may not have an operational role, will often delegate the task of leadership to the manager. The head chef may work as an equal with a manager or report directly to the manager. The head chef is also the leader of the kitchen staff.

Management is doing things right. Leadership is doing the right things.

No management success can compensate for failure in leadership. If what looks like an opportunity does not advance the strategic goals of the institution, it is not an opportunity, it is a distraction.

Peter Drucker
Management Challenges for the 21st Century

Management theory. Modern management theory abounds with the analysis of business leaders and their particular style of leadership. Students of history will know that the past is peppered with great names that are remembered well beyond the circumstances that led to their fame. During the 20th century leadership has become democratised. Political leadership that centred around a hereditary wealthy elite has been replaced. The *American Dream* where the penniless child becomes a millionaire-president is a truth of this age. Imbued with intelligence, wit and a sense of destiny, the pauper can become the prince. Part of this democratisation has been that leadership is no longer an exclusive skill. Leadership can be learnt and courses around the world share this knowledge. From corporates to small businesses leadership affects us all.

> **An effective leader should be:**
> 1. Able to set the direction and maintain the focus
> 2. Able to build a competent, motivated team
> 3. A good manager

Hold a vision. As we discussed in Chapter Three, it is important to understand where you are headed; *to begin with the end in mind*. A leader must be able to communicate this vision to others and together they will patiently pursue it. The leader must always look ahead for new opportunities and challenges and have the courage to take risks. A leader needs energy. If you relish the hard work and feel stimulated by the challenge, your optimism will enthuse those around you.

Power. Leadership is often defined as power and the ability to influence others. *Personal power* relates to your personality, your charisma and therefore your ability to convince others to support you. Power can also be derived from your position *(positional power)*. You may be the local chairman of a political party or the chief executive of a multinational corporation. Losing the position would result in you losing your power. As David Lange commented, *the phone stops ringing*. Employers have power when a person is employed by them, but once the person leaves the job, the power goes. *Expert power* is when you develop knowledge in an area that makes you an expert. A forensic psychologist in a murder trial has power because of their expertise and not because of their personality.

The behavior of a leader is often broken down into a number of categories. *Authoritarian or autocratic style* is where the leader is in control and determines what is to be done and how it should be done. This person often remains aloof and does not seek advice from others. *Democratic or participative* leadership occurs when the leader allows the team to participate in the decision-making process. A *permissive* leader is characterised by someone who is nice to everyone and dislikes confrontation. A *transformational* leader provides the catalyst that enables the transformation of people by sowing the seeds of creativity and providing the opportunity for personal growth and development.

Styles of leadership. Within each leader there is the ability to demonstrate all these of styles of leadership at different times. While participative leaders make the team feel valued and involved, on occasions it is important for the leader to be decisive which may seem autocratic. Often the leader has more in-depth knowledge of the problem or is more focused on the strategic vision. Participative leadership can result in a *watered-down* version where the team seeks to accommodate the concerns of all the individuals. This can result in poor decisions and lack of commitment to the true vision of the organisation. It is at this point that a leader must assert the right to veto and say *"No, that is a good idea, but it is not in line with our long term vision"*. Sometimes leadership can be achieved in subtle ways; for example, where the leader pursues the goals quietly in the background. I do not mean this in a manipulative sense, but the leader who holds the vision will understand how to work towards it.

Trust. Leadership is primarily about trust and establishing your integrity. Your team must bestow their trust in you to lead them. A leader who is not trusted will only succeed by coercion. Stephen Covey[2] talks about the *emotional bank account*, a metaphor for the amount of trust that has been built up in a relationship. You make deposits by addressing little details, being kind and understanding, giving positive feedback, thanking someone or apologising when you have made a mistake. You make withdrawals when you overreact, snap, threaten or become arbitrary.

A chef under pressure may yell and castigate other staff, leaving them upset and unsure of what they are supposed to do. By denigrating an assistant in front of the other staff, the assistant feels wounded, unsure of how they can correct their mistake and their confidence evaporates. They may feel unfairly treated and withdraw their support for the chef, resulting in a decline in their personal performance. The emotional bank balance is over-drawn.

Listen. Successful leaders are good at listening. Covey goes on to explain the importance of listening.[3] We must learn to *listen with our eyes* as your body radiates how you feel. We normally listen at one of five levels. The first is by *ignoring* what is being said. The second is by *pretending to listen*.

The third level is *selective listening* when you hear only certain parts of the conversation, such as the chatter of a child. The fourth level is *attentive listening* when you pay attention only to the words. What we really need to do is become *empathic listeners*. This occurs when you listen with the intention of understanding what is being said from the other person's point of view. You listen by observing them as well as hearing the words. By listening empathetically you demonstrate respect for the other person.

Self-confidence. Leadership is also about self-confidence. As we age we become more confident and at ease with our opinions and views. For some it takes courage to stand up in front of a group of people and say what you think. Confidence does not need to be boisterous or demanding. It should be balanced with humility.

Leadership can be extremely testing. A leader can be forced to delve deeply into their internal reserves to make a difficult decision and then find the strength to act. Leadership can transform a person by extending them way beyond what they thought they were capable of. A leader must develop a sense of detachment to be able to step back, analyse, re-group, reinvent and re-motivate. The leader must also find fortitude to withstand personal criticism and take solace from Kipling's words, *"If you can keep your head when all about you are losing theirs and blaming it on you"*.

Self-awareness. It is important to be sufficiently self-analytical to understand yourself and what motivates you. Many tools exist to do this. Besides reading a horoscope each day, you can also be appraised by a Myers Briggs test, or a host of other personality appraisal methods. They will look at you and how you rate in terms of your personality and decision-making style. Developing a sense of self-awareness can take time and discipline. To be an effective leader however, you need to understand how other people react to you and if necessary, learn to change. Having a sense of humour to laugh along with others, as well as at yourself, is a great asset.

Personal development. Everybody needs to renew their commitment to an organisation and replenish their reserves of energy. If you feel personally fulfilled you will do a much better job at everything. Rediscover the joy of learning. Knowledge and the access to new knowledge is frequently cited as a means by which people keep interested in their careers. Devise a personal development plan for yourself. This may involve attending a course or conference or even reading a book. Knowledge is power. It inspires a new perspective with new ideas.

Conflict. Conflict in any organisation can be very destructive. Individual conflict often arises as a result of the interaction between different personalities. Group conflict can be far more insidious and may result in the group failing to perform. Work can be difficult. The leader can feel isolated and misunderstood. When a problem is identified it needs to be resolved as soon as possible, even if you do not want to deal with it. Being decisive and facing up to the problems when they first emerge will avoid the anguish that may result if the problem is allowed to fester.

Change. For many people, change is a fearful prospect. Routines differ, new staff are appointed and the group dynamics alter. Suspicion and rumour can create havoc. Change needs to be managed in a positive way. Informing people from the outset about the changes and your new vision can alleviate many of the issues. They want to know what to expect. A leader needs to create a *holding environment* where staff understand what is happening and trust your judgement sufficiently to work through the process of change.

Delegation. For a business to grow the owner must be able to delegate to others. Delegation is about sharing the responsibilities. It takes confidence to delegate, and therefore, you need to make sure that staff are sufficiently trained and understand what is expected of them. Delegation gives others a chance to develop more skills and can provide a reward for good work. For delegation to be successful you need to explain precisely what is to be done and the outcome expected. It is always a good idea to give a deadline so that the person knows exactly the time frame they must work to.

BUILDING A TEAM. A team is a group of individuals with complementary skills committed to a common purpose with common performance goals that they are collectively accountable for.[4] Teams can achieve goals more effectively and efficiently than an individual working alone. A collection of diverse individuals brings a variety of skills and new ideas. Learning to harness the energies of an assortment of personalities can be one of the greatest challenges facing a new leader. Your team members must become your greatest advocates. *Everyone walks the talk.* If the team upholds and endorses the product and the organisation, it motivates them and gives the customers confidence.

Organisational structure. In the past, larger organisations were characterised by multiple levels of authority. For a decision to be made, it needed to be approved by a number of different people at different levels. While that situation may still apply to some of the bigger hospitality businesses, like the hotels and casinos, for the smaller businesses, smallness is an advantage. To pursue innovation, you need to be able to make a fast response. A flat organisational structure with limited levels of authority is much more flexible than the hierarchical design. An *organic* structure allows a *free-flow* of information between levels, with a low degree of formal rules and procedures. A *mechanistic* structure has a more formal structure with rules and firmly designated roles. As Peter Drucker[5] comments, an organisation that is transparent and with fewer layers will not suffer from the situation where "...*every relay doubles the noise and cuts the message in half*".

Establishing a culture. Even in a small organisation a culture exists. It is a vague term that relates to consensus amongst the group about their values and behaviour. It encapsulates an attitude or a spirit about the organisation. With well-established teams, there are specific symbols of identity, such as stories of past events or annual traditions. A sense of culture heightens the individual's commitment to the organisation. They feel part of it, identify with its values and become its greatest defenders. The staff of the Dux de Lux, a Christchurch bar and restaurant, have a well-organised social calendar culminating with their legendary Christmas party. The Dux employs a lot of students, who come to Christchurch from around the country and are drawn to seek jobs there because of its reputation. The culture is strong and while it does centre around the leader, the culture has developed its own humour and traditions.

Rewards. How you reward staff requires consideration. If you see the position purely as hourly work for hourly pay, you will create an environment of clock-watchers with little commitment beyond their designated hours. To attract, motivate and retain competent employees, firstly they must receive an *economic reward* that recognises their skills and competencies. On top of this they require an emotional reward or recognition for the work done. The *emotional reward* gives satisfaction to the individual. This is often the reason that people volunteer for unpaid work.

Feedback. Thomas Connellean[6] in his book on Disney talks of three types of feedback. As well as positive and negative feedback, which we understand, he describes the absence of feedback as extinction. This is when you get neither positive nor negative comments. You do not know what people think about you or how you do your job. The absence of feedback can cause people to withdraw their commitment to whatever they are doing. They feel that they are not valued and do not know why. Extinction can be just as devastating as negative feedback.

Performance regularly goes unnoticed and unacknowledged. Recognising someone's effort shows that you are aware of their contribution and this makes the person feel valued. The feedback should not come six months after the event. The best feedback is now when it is current and relevant to the task at hand.

> *"I like what you did ..."*
> *"That looks great ..."*
> *"I appreciate the effort you made ..."*
> *"Thanks for staying late to help me ..."*

Negative feedback needs to given in private. Telling off people in front of their colleagues can be very destructive. They feel embarrassed, self-conscious and angry at the humiliation. They may respond in anger. It is far better to go somewhere private to discuss the problem. You must always be sincere and consider the words that you use. Your negotiation skills and ability to read body language will help you resolve the problem.

> *"I have a problem over ..."*
> *"I am not happy about ..."*
> *"I am concerned about ..."*

Appraisals. Assessing performance is one of the most powerful tools that a manager has. A formal job appraisal enables the manager to review the performance of a person. If handled properly it can leave the employer and employee happy and enhance their relationship. It can be a time of mutual feedback and when new goals are determined. I use this time to talk about the person's career path and where they are headed. We may identify training and personal development needs. It is usually in these discussions that staff will indicate if they are planning to leave. By being open about the fact that there will come a point when the staff member wishes to move on, we are able to manage the replacement process. Frequently people will tell me in October that they want to leave in April. This gives us six months to plan for the succession.

Lack of motivation. When staff are unmotivated it is often more a comment on the leader than a reflection on the individuals. It often stems from a failure to acknowledge and reward the person's performance. New projects and challenges keep people interested. Understanding the individual motivations of your team will offer ideas of how you can apportion work. Absenteeism as well as illness are often symptoms of lack of commitment.

HOW TO NEGOTIATE. Every day we negotiate. It may be something simple like an extra hour for lunch or something complex such as a legal dispute. An effective leader must understand the nuances of negotiation.

Our legal system is designed to produce winners and losers *(I win – you lose)* or a 50/50 settlement *(I lose – you lose)* where neither side is happy. If you are the winner you feel happy; if you lose you can feel bitter and resentful. In recent years there has been a trend towards a negotiated settlement which is designed to take into account the feelings of both sides and produce a settlement that is agreeable to both. This is often called the *win-win* approach *(I win – you win)*.[7]

Negotiation often takes one of three approaches. A *soft* negotiation avoids personal conflict and can be amicable, with participants parting as friends. However often this type of negotiation can result in one side feeling exploited *(I lose – you win)*.

> *"I don't want to argue – you win. But I'm really upset."*
> *"I don't want to argue – you win. But I'm only doing this to be kind."*
> *"I don't want to argue – you win. But I'm only doing this for the kids."*

A *hard* negotiation is a contest of wills and the method most commonly used by the legal profession. It often produces an equally hard response in the opponent. Sometimes the weaker party backs off and gives in to the other side to prevent any more harm. Hard negotiations can result in the participants parting as adversaries. The *principled approach*[8] looks at the issues on their merits. Mutual gain is sought *(win-win)*. A wise outcome is reached amicably. The principled approach attempts to separate people from the problems *(soft on people, hard on problems)*. There is no contest of wills nor can there be positioning, posturing, stand-over tactics or deceit.

Characteristics of a negotiation. In a negotiation, if there appears to be just one issue this can be extremely polarising. When there are a number of issues there is more to talk about. Once the negotiation has started, it can be difficult to get a deal. People are more creative at the start of negotiations and can be more receptive to making a deal. This also happens when the end of the negotiation is in sight.

Try to understand the other party and what their preferences are. If you know what is important to them, you may be able to find common ground where you can negotiate. Avoid threats. They are counter-productive and often indicate that you do not want to go through with this action. An implicit threat is much more powerful than one that has been specified. By avoiding a hard view from the outset, you leave yourself open to more solutions.

Sometimes the best strategy is to *cut your losses* and settle. The further you go in a negotiation, the more you get locked into your position. If you employ professional advisors, there can be huge costs. There is also an emotional cost. As the process gathers its own momentum and your commitment escalates, you are less able to accept losses. Losses are about loss of face, humiliation and anger. It is at this point that you wish to *inflict maximum damage*. The situation can turn into a battle of egos with the original issue becoming irrelevant. Arguments distort our ability to listen.

HOW TO RUN A SUCCESSFUL MEETING. I spent three years as a district councillor for the Banks Peninsula District. It was an interesting experience and I came away with a much better understanding of how to run successful meetings. A meeting is a powerful communication tool whether it is for a political purpose or not. Many people however, do not know how to use it effectively. There is nothing worse than a chairperson or facilitator who lacks direction and is unable to hold the meeting together. The meetings tend to be long drawn-out affairs and the participants get frustrated at the lack of progress. The meeting stalls.

In government there are standing orders that set out the rules and procedures for running a meeting. These include matters such as apologies, ensuring a quorum, reading of the minutes of the previous meeting and the passing of resolutions. In a less formal situation it is not necessary to have such a structure. However for meetings to be successful some structure is needed.

Structure. A meeting should always commence at the designated time and there should be some consensus as to its length. Meetings will otherwise just run on and on. An agenda should be determined beforehand or set out at the beginning of the meeting. Some ground rules should be established. There should be agreement on how decisions will be made; for instance, will there need to be a vote? While the chairperson or facilitator is a participant, they should not dominate the discussion. All the participants should be encouraged to contribute. This will foster a richer dialogue and more ideas. There should be consensus that the participants will respect each other and listen to what they have to say without the fear of interjections.

The facilitator. The facilitator must drive the meeting and ensure that it is moving along and not getting stalled on an issue. A facilitator must be able to summarise the discussion and gain some consensus on the progress. The body language of the participants will give the facilitator a very good idea about what they are feeling. If they are slumped in their seats and silent, chances are, they are not very happy. When participants start repeating what has already been said, it is time to move forward. A written record should be made of the discussion and conclusions summarised in an action plan.

Personal attributes of effective leaders
- Hold a vision and understand the strategy to achieve it.
- Find fortitude to withstand personal criticism.
- Be a good manager with sound financial and administrative skills.
- Demonstrate integrity, honesty, a sense of fairness and compassion. Be self-aware.
- Be able to build and motivate a team to support you and trust you.
- Be a good communicator.
- Learn to listen and read body language.
- Understand how to negotiate.
- Have a sense of humour.
- Show patience and commitment to the task.
- Have the courage to take risks.
- Keep detached; step back, analyse, regroup, reinvent, re-motivate

1. Peters, T. *The Circle of Innovation*, 1997.
2. Covey, S. *The 7 Habits of Highly Effective People*, 1989.
3. Covey, S. *The 7 Habits of Highly Effective People*, 1989.
4. *Harvard Managementor*, Leading a Team, 1998.
5. Drucker, P. *Management Challenges of the 20th Century*, 1999.
6. Connellan, T. *Inside the Magic Kingdom*, 1966.
7. For a comprehensive discussion on the Win-Win approach refer to Covey, S. *The 7 Habits of Highly Effective People*, 1989.
8. Fisher, R. and Ury, W. *Getting to Yes*, 2nd ed., 1991.

CHAPTER EIGHT

EMPLOYING THE RIGHT PEOPLE

For a new manager or owner, the hiring process can be one of the most difficult decisions. In this chapter, we look at how to hire staff and the skills and responsibilities of key positions in the organisation. If you get it right, it will result in a better performance by your team and business. Getting it wrong can be expensive, time-consuming and stressful.

Diners shouldn't ever feel insulted or ignored, and the restaurant experience should begin at the entrance and continue until the customer leaves. Good service means looking after the customer's needs, even when the customers are demanding.

Lauraine Jacobs, Cuisine Restaurant Guide

The hospitality industry employs many people just to keep the place serviced and customers happy. No machine can do this task. While much has been made of the lack of professionalism in this industry, this is more an indictment of management than the staff employed. Employers argue that their staff members do not see the job as a long-term career prospect. I feel that this is irrelevant. What is needed is a commitment to do a good job and take pleasure in that. I have had excellent staff, many working part-time as students, who have viewed waiting as a *transition* job but have still taken pride each day in their responsibilities. Professionalism comes down to staff training. Instilling a genuine love of learning in each staff member will result in them developing and looking for ways to improve their skills and knowledge.

How many people. It is impossible to make broad generalisation about the number of staff required for a business to operate. A fine dining restaurant may need more staff per customer than a café. A seven-day operation that opens day and night may run two or three eight-hour shifts which all need to be fully staffed. For most hospitality businesses it is difficult to gauge the level of staff required from one night to the next and this is the reason why so many part-time and casual staff are employed. At Hay's, to run the restaurant during the day we would need two staff working front of house and two chefs in the kitchen. During a busy dinner service of 65 diners, we would have three waiting staff plus a runner as well as someone to clear plates and help polish cutlery. The kitchen would have three chefs and one dishwasher. Not all of these positions are full-time and the junior chefs and runner would only work on average four hours per night.

Job analysis. Any recruitment process starts with a job analysis that identifies the skills required to successfully perform the job. It is also essential to understand the personal attributes that will enable a successful candidate to adapt to the culture of the organisation. In general, a manager would be required to conduct job interviews and make the job offer. The job description formalises the job analysis in a written format. Analysing the job will paint a picture of the most desirable candidate and this will help when it comes to selecting whom to interview.

Job analysis
1. Job title
2. Job purpose
3. Reporting relationships
4. Level of authority
5. Pay and benefits
6. Hours
7. Educational prerequisites
8. Experience/skills/competencies
9. Personal characteristics: interpersonal skills, decision making ability
10. Job responsibilities

EMPLOYING THE MANAGER. The manager is in a leadership role and this job often involves recruiting all other staff, including the head chef. In some organisations the chef and the manager may have equal status, employ their own staff and report to the owner or area manager. The delegation of tasks between those two roles must be specific to avoid conflict between the holders of the positions. In a large organisation, the manager may not have a front of house role and may employ duty managers, who hold their Sale of Liquor manager's licence.

The *maitre d'hôtel* is the manager in a French restaurant. The *maitre d'* would be supported by assistants (*chefs de rang*) and a *sommelier*. The *sommelier* is responsible for the selection of the wine list and may have his own staff serving the wine to diners. In New Zealand, only the larger hotels or fine-dining restaurants employ a *sommelier*. Often the responsibilities of developing a wine list falls on the manager who may in turn delegate this to another staff member. A manager may train the waiting staff to perform both functions of food and wine service.

The manager's role is both a sales position and a public relations one. The manager is the public face of the business and therefore needs to be visible. The manager should be the organisation's best sales person and take responsibility for training staff to ensure they are knowledgeable and efficient. While I do not work every night in the restaurant, I try to be there at least two or three nights a week. Even if I am not needed to help with dinner service, I always make a special effort to chat to people. I am always pleased that I do as I always learn something and I get feedback about the experience at Hay's. I am also able to conduct my own market research by asking international visitors where they are from, where they are staying and how they heard about us.

Business administration and awareness. A manager should understand the administrative side of the business. This includes filing, creditors/debtors, wages, PAYE, cash book, GST and stocktake procedures. Even if the firm employs someone else to do this administration, having a manager who is business-aware and has a general knowledge of the legislation affecting business is a real benefit. Computer skills should be part of a manager's basket of tools. Computers enable a manager to do things such as devise a costing schedule in a spreadsheet or to write a quote for a function. An effective manager must understand the relationship between income and profit. They must know how the business makes money and acknowledge their role in helping in this process.

Attention to detail. A good manager knows that it is important to take pride in how the restaurant looks. Cleaning schedules need to be established to ensure the place is clean and tidy and fittings are well-maintained. The ordering of stock for the front of house needs to be done regularly, especially beverages to ensure that the wine list is accurate. Like the chef, the manager needs to understand food, personal hygiene and the safety aspects of the business.

Staff theft. Part of the manager's job is security and in particular staff theft. Large bars, restaurants and cafés with lots of staff and high sales can be easy targets. Theft ranges from a staff member not charging friends for drinks, to pocketing the money without ringing in the sale on the cash register. Credit card theft occurs in a number of ways. One example is when a staff member enters a higher amount for the transaction, on the assumption that the customer will not check the docket, and then takes the extra money in cash. Some businesses suffer from staff bringing in their own spirits, pouring them into empty bottles of more expensive brands and taking the authentic product home. Theft can also occur when staff help themselves to plates, cutlery, uniforms or even toilet paper!

Large bars will often resort to security cameras above the bar area and increasingly cameras are used in big restaurants to monitor the front of house. The key to minimising staff theft is to ensure there are procedures in place that reduce the temptation to steal. Procedures for handling cash need to be explained during the induction process. Little things like not allowing staff to ring in their own transactions can prevent theft. Weekly stock takes will soon show if theft is occurring because the gross profit percentage will not be achieved. Strict guidelines on what staff can eat and drink is also essential. Many bars will *shout* a drink after the service or offer generous staff discounts to avoid staff helping themselves.

Restaurant manager responsibilities

1. *To lead the front of house staff*
   Objective: To build a team that is efficient, effective, knowledgeable and supportive of the manager.
   - To demonstrate a commitment to customer service.
   - To demonstrate good interpersonal skills.
   - To demonstrate a commitment to on-going training.
   - To organise and delegate daily routines, cleaning rosters, setting up.
   - To develop wine/beer/spirit lists and order stock.

2. *Business administration and awareness skills*
   Objective: To ensure that the business survives.
   - To demonstrate sound business management skills.
   - To maintain a clean, tidy and hygienic restaurant/café that meets the requirements of Health and Safety legislation.
   - To understand other legislation that affects business.
   - To roster staff to a level that is within the wages budget.
   - To recognise the importance of making a profit.

The manager may also be responsible for employing and training the front of house staff. Some staff will be expected to come in before the business opens to set it up while others will be expected to remain to clean up after the last customers have gone. The outline below lists the basic skills that you would expect from a front of house person to perform their job effectively.

Front of house – waiting position

Responsible to the manager
Major Responsibilities:
1. *Retail sales and waiting skills*
   Objective: To consistently practise the principles of excellent customer service.
   • Serving customer needs in a friendly, efficient and enthusiastic manner.
   • Anticipating and exceeding customer needs.

2. *Setting up the restaurant/café for the meal service*
   Objective: To ensure a clean and attractively presented café.
   • Stocking wine/beer refrigerators.
   • Setting tables.
   • Cleaning.

3. *Personal appearance*
   Objective: To present a clean and tidy appearance to the customers.
   • Wear the prescribed uniform.
   • Be clean and tidy.

EMPLOYING THE HEAD CHEF/CHEF DE CUISINE. When recruiting for a head chef position it is important to define exactly what you want the chef to do. As with all staff, failure to communicate your expectations at the outset can result in misunderstandings. This job can be stressful. The kitchen is hot and noisy and it can be hard to hear others above the roar of the extraction fan. It is a charged atmosphere. The chef must work hard and fast. The chef's patience is tested. Not everyone has the temperament to withstand the pressure of a busy dinner service. If you are looking for a head chef to lead your team it is important to ensure they can stand the heat!

Until the late 1980s the New Zealand chefs qualification was based on the English City and Guilds Diploma. This was then replaced by the Trade Certificate in Professional Cookery which consisted of Basic Cookery Certificate 751, General Catering Certificate 752 and Professional Cookery Certificate

753. Today we see applicants with a mixture of these certificates. The Professional Cookery series has now been replaced with the National Certificate in Hospitality – Cookery, which is unit standard based. Many Polytechnics now offer a combination of City and Guilds and unit standards. In New Zealand a qualified chef is someone who has passed 753 or the City and Guilds Diploma; however many people who call themselves "chef", do not have either of these qualifications. For a business manager, it is often very difficult to ascertain how skilled an applicant is.

There are still lots of chefs who are not good cooks. They may talk knowledgeably and with confidence but it is only in the kitchen that you can see if the talk matches the skills. This is particularly true for menu design. One measure is to assess them on a *Gourmand Scale*. By this I mean to evaluate how dedicated they are to continue to learn about new ideas, new recipes and new ingredients. Brillat-Savarin, the French culinary commentator in 1825, described gourmandism as *the impassioned, reasoned and habitual preference for everything which gratifies the organ of taste.*[1]

Assessing on the *Gourmand Scale*							How do you rate?	
1. Does not read food publications					Dedicated follower of food publications			
1	2	3	4	5	6	7	8	9
Apathetic							Passionate	
2. Does not experiment at home						Enjoys experimenting		
1	2	3	4	5	6	7	8	9
Apathetic							Passionate	
3. Does not eat out					Enjoys eating out and trying new foods			
1	2	3	4	5	6	7	8	9
Apathetic							Passionate	
4. Uses same recipes/ingredients		Constantly looking for new ingredients and recipes						
1	2	3	4	5	6	7	8	9
Apathetic							Passionate	
5. Will drive all over town to purchase the best ingredients								
1	2	3	4	5	6	7	8	9
Apathetic							Passionate	
6. Uses the same ingredients								
1	2	3	4	5	6	7	8	9
Apathetic							Passionate	

The chef as a leader. A chef needs to understand the role of the team leader and how to build trust and support from the staff. The interpersonal skills of the chef can make or break the team. The chef's responsibilities also include staffing and determining the weekly kitchen rosters. The impact of the power of the customer has also reached the kitchen. A chef must listen to the customers and respect their opinions.

Designing the menu. The chef should be able to create a menu that reflects the personality of the business. This includes sourcing products and costing the menu to the food cost ratio specifications. Menus are the glamorous side of the job. It involves putting the chef's mark on the restaurant or café; making a personal statement for the customers to appraise. Every chef wants to design the menu but not every chef has the skills, although they may think that they do!

Mis en place. The preparation for the meal service is a crucial job. Time management skills are important and chefs must be able to work efficiently to ensure the preparation is completed before the service. There is nothing more frustrating than watching a chef finish meal preparation during the dinner service which in turn delays the presentation of the meals to the waiting customers.

General management. A chef must be aware of the kitchen's responsibilities in the process of making a profit to ensure that the business survives. The chef is a manager and needs to learn the skills of management. This is an area of personal development that the chef may wish to pursue. It is important that the chef understands the costs of wages to avoid overstaffing. As your confidence grows in the chef it is possible to delegate the responsibility of recruiting new kitchen staff. However remember to provide training in recruitment with special focus on Employment Law.

A chef's responsibilities usually include stock control. It is essential that the chef grasps the importance of stock rotation and not holding too much stock at any one time. Most kitchens work on J.I.T. or the *Just in time* model of inventory control where they order only what they need and do not hold large stocks. The head chef is also responsible for ensuring the restaurant or café kitchen meets the standards required by the Environmental Health and Safety regulations. A chef must know the basic rules of food hygiene.

The list below is a summary of the responsibilities that may be expected of a chef.

Summary of head chef responsibilities
1. *To lead the kitchen staff*
    Objective: To build an efficient and supportive team.
    - To demonstrate a commitment to customer service.
    - To demonstrate good interpersonal skills.
    - To demonstrate a commitment to on-going training.
    - To organise and delegate daily routines, cleaning rosters.
    - To roster staff to a level that is within the wages budget.

2. *Designing the menu*
   Objective: To create a menu that reflects the style of the establishment and is within the food cost budget.

3. *Mis en place and cooking of meals*
   Objective: To ensure that meals are prepared and presented to a consistently high standard.

4. *Maintaining a safe and hygienic environment*
   Objective: To maintain a clean kitchen, which complies with safety and hygiene standards at all times.

5. *Ordering supplies*
   Objective: To ensure that minimum stocks are held.
   To ensure that all goods are delivered in a fit condition.

6. *Customer awareness*
   Objective: Develop an understanding of the importance of the customer.

7. *Business awareness*
   Objective: Recognise the importance of making a profit to ensure that the business survives.

Assistant chef/cook. The number of assistant cooks/chefs will depend on the size of the kitchen and the customer demand for the restaurant or café. In a large kitchen, a *sous chef* will be employed as the assistant to the head chef. The *sous chef* should be capable of running the kitchen in the chef's absence. Smaller kitchens may not have a *sous chef* but employ someone temporarily when the chef is sick or on holiday. An assistant chef, often called a *commis*, performs functions designated by the chef. These will vary considerably. They might include vegetable preparation, trimming meat, dessert preparation, soups and breads. During the service they may be responsible for cooking and presenting the soups and starters and perhaps the desserts. They may help the chef *plate up* by preparing the vegetables to partner the meat that the chef cooks.

Summary of assistant chef skills
Responsible to head chef

1. *Demonstrate sound cooking skills*
   Objective: To ensure that meals are prepared and presented to a consistently high standard.

2. *Follow instructions of the head chef*
   Objective: To build a supportive and efficient team.

3. *Demonstrate a willingness to learn new skills*
   Objective: To develop skills and increase abilities with the goal of taking on increased responsibilities.

4. *Kitchen cleaning and safety*
   Objective: To maintain a clean kitchen that complies with safety and hygiene standards at all times.

5. *Personal appearance*
   Objective: To maintain professional standards.

6. *Customer awareness*
   Objective: To develop an understanding of the importance of the customer.

FLASH POINTS. The manager and the head chef must be able to work together to run an effective team. So often tensions between the front of house and the kitchen undermine this. For both the chef and manager it is important to understand the pressures of the other's job and respect the role that each plays in fulfilling the customer's needs. The discussion below describes some of the flash points that occur.

Disagreement on the menu design
Chef feels that his/her professional integrity is undermined.
Manager feels chef does not understand the customers/market.

Food costs over budget
Chef feels that the manager is undermining his creativity.
Manager feels chef does not understand the need to make a profit.

Wage costs over budget
Chef feels that manager does not understand how difficult it is
to prepare the food.
Manager feels that chef over-staffs because:
- Chef does not like to do the work.
- Chef does not care about profitability.
- Chef has made the menu too complicated.

Disorganisation in the kitchen
Chef feels this is his/her space and the manager should not interfere.
Manager feels that disorganisation is evidence of chef's poor management.
Manager feels that chef treats the staff badly.

Busy dinner service where customers wait too long for their meal
Chef feels manager does not understand the pressure chef is under.
Manager feels that chef is not up to the job.

Mistakes on dockets
Chef feels that the waiters are incompetent and treats them badly.
Manager is upset at the way chef treats the waiters.

Customer complains about the quality of food
Chef feels that the quality is fine and the customer is being difficult.
Manager feels that the customer has a point but chef will not listen.

Customer complains about the quality of service
Chef feels the front of house is letting the restaurant down.
Manager feels that chef should support the team rather than
siding with the customer.

Support and respect
Chef feels he/she works hard and that the manager gives no support/respect.
Manager feels that he/she works hard and that the chef gives no
support/respect.

FINDING THE RIGHT STAFF. When recruiting, my first choice is always to
look within the organisation to see if there is someone suitable to fill the role.
It is important for your current staff to feel that they have not been passed
over. It also offers them an opportunity to further develop their own careers.
I regularly get asked if we have New Zealand School of Food and Wine
graduates that are looking for work. Sometimes we have suitable candidates

and other times we do not. It is always a good idea to approach a training institute to see if there are students available. Putting a sign in the window is another technique. This results in a mixture of responses but essentially you are limited to those people walking past. Recruitment agencies that specialise in hospitality placements offer another resource and will charge a fee for this service. Shoulder tapping, where you approach someone that you know and offer them a job, can be a very convenient way to recruit.

With all these methods you have limited your choice of candidates. To reach the greatest market for candidates, you must advertise in the situations vacant in your local newspaper. The Saturday paper is the best way to reach the largest number of people. With increasing use of the Internet this too will offer an avenue of recruitment, but you will miss all the people who are not computer literate!

Writing an advertisement. Sometimes it is hard to write copy for advertisements. The best way is to pretend that you are the reader. Be cheeky. Write an ad that captures the reader's imagination. When you put energy into your ads, it will stimulate an inspired response. Your advertising copy cannot contain words that may breach the Human Rights Act. This means that you cannot state a preference for age, gender, marital status, religious belief, ethical beliefs, political opinion, colour, race, ethnic origin, disability, employment status, family status or sexual orientation. Say who you are. Anonymous ads are for the big head hunters trying to recruit for big institutions. If you are a café and you are proud of that, it achieves nothing by concealing that information.

Writing an advertisement
The first sentence should have impact.
Keep the ad short and focused.
Describe the position.
What skills are you are after?
Specify the approximate hours and days of the week.
Please apply in writing enclosing a CV.
Your name
The organisation
Address
Closing date for applications

Apply in writing. Ads that give a telephone number often result in the telephone line being engaged for hours while your valued customers are unable to get through. It is difficult to interview over the phone when one of the prerequisites is that the person be well-presented. The risk is that you have to see everyone just to sort out the good prospects. A written application shows the applicant's motivation to compose a letter and put something in the post. It also gives you the opportunity to see whether the person is literate. A curriculum vitae (CV) is standard practice. This gives the employer an opportunity to digest information about the candidate in advance. It should list the applicant's work history and offer several references. Often it answers questions that are difficult to ask such as the candidate's age and work history.

Reference checking. Some people choose to check references before they actually see the candidate. I tend to do it after the interview. Sometimes with young people I do not bother. With experience, it is easy to tell whether or not they will respond to training. A reference check would probably put you off. Often what young people need is a chance to develop their own work ethic and that will only happen by working in a stable, supportive environment with good work practices.

SELECTION FOR INTERVIEW. Overwhelmed by the response to your ad, the first step is to evaluate each candidate for the basic skills required. The importance of the applicant's letter is apparent here. The letter should convince the reader that the candidate must have an interview. The first cull can be quick. If you focus on the skills identified in the job analysis, it is easy to eliminate candidates.
- *Does the candidate have the skills required?*
- *Does the candidate sound motivated and interested?*
- *Does this job match the candidate's career path?*
- *Is the candidate too well qualified?*
- *Can you see evidence of achievement in a previous job or at college?*

The goal should be to get a short list of 4–8 candidates. Interviewing too many people at one time is exhausting. Your questioning becomes stale and unless you are good at taking notes, there is a tendency to confuse your impression of each applicant. You will remember the first and last applicants. The length of the interview will vary depending on how important the job is. Interviews for a dishwasher or junior waiting staff may only take ten minutes. Interviews for a chef or front of house manager should take at least thirty minutes and a second interview may be needed. Telephone screening is a good way to clarify information submitted by the candidate and help decide whether to interview them or not.

At a second interview, the candidate is more relaxed. At this stage it is good to involve other senior staff members who may have to work directly with the person. For important jobs in large organisations a personality or work sample test may be carried out by a professional human resources consultant. This is to demonstrate the skills and aptitude of the candidate. In the hospitality industry it is common for candidates to be asked to complete unpaid work experience in the job. This is may be for a period of up to three days. After this point a job offer should be made or the person should be paid for the work done. Some organisations will ask a chef to prepare a meal for the manager or head chef. This gives the chef the opportunity to demonstrate their skills in cooking and presentation. This enables the employer to assess the applicant's work habits and to see whether they fit into the organisation. The candidate must always be informed that this is work experience and they will not be paid for it. Unless you specifically state this, it could lead to confusion and expectation of payment.

Warning signs. Candidates who have little experience often overemphasise their educational achievements. An employer is not interested in every certificate or grade that an applicant has gained during their life. Look for unexplained gaps in the applicant's employment history. If no references are included, this could indicate that the applicant has something to hide. Typing errors often indicate poor attention to detail. It is important to acknowledge all applications, even if it is a letter of decline. This at least recognises the effort that an applicant has gone to. The applicant may be a future customer!

Personal biases. Be aware of your own biases towards information such as the candidate's school or qualifications, or how you may feel about their former employer. Do not judge someone negatively just because they remind you of someone you do not like. Remember the *10-second rule* which means that people are judged on first impressions. The candidate then has several minutes to change that impression before the interviewer reverts to their original judgement.

Common lapses of judgement
- Trying to employ clones of yourself.
- Employing someone who reminds you of someone you like.
- Being too impressed by:
  1. Previous work experience.
  2. School, university or polytechnic attended.
  3. Qualifications gained.
  4. The ability to talk knowledgeably about something they do not know much about.
  5. The ability to talk knowledgeably about something you do not know much about, especially using French terms to describe their cooking.

Erroneous Beliefs
- All part-time student staff will not offer a professional service.
- All part-time student staff are not committed to doing a good job.
- All young people lack the maturity to do a manager's job.
- All quiet people lack motivation.

THE INTERVIEW. The interview is the opportunity for both the applicant and the interviewer to share information. From the job analysis it is possible to devise a set of questions to ask. This will help determine whether the candidate has the skills to match the job requirements. The questions give a structure and enable the interviewer to ask the same questions of each applicant. Within this structure it is good to deviate as the interview progresses so that you can follow along an unexpected tangent. You can always refer to the questions to help focus and keep you on track. Be familiar with the relevant points of the CV before the candidate arrives.

The first step is to establish eye contact and acknowledge the person while using open body language. Let the candidate sit so they feel comfortable. A clip-board with the resumé and your summary of questions is a good idea. Tell the candidate that you intend to take notes, but be judicious so that they do not think that you are writing everything down. This can be very disconcerting and can result in the candidate not talking fully. Nodding, smiling, and laughing will exact a better response than if you offer no feedback.

You must feel comfortable with silence while you wait for the candidate's response. Long silences make people feel uncomfortable. However, sometimes you just need to be patient and not feel that you need to fill the silence with talk.

Style of Questions. Questions must be *open-ended* rather than leading which forces the candidate to answer in a particular way. The best questions start with *What? How? Why? When? Where?* Let the candidate do the talking. Avoid questions that start with *Did? Do?* and *Are?* These words result in yes/no answers. Avoid questions that the person may have ethical difficulties answering. Under the Privacy Act you cannot ask a candidate's age, sexual orientation, marital status, number of children, religion, or weight. Beware of questions in which the candidate will answer with the answer that they believe you want to hear. These are referred to as socially desirable answers.

Socially desirable answers
How do you cope with stress in the kitchen?
I handle stress well.

How do you cope with deadlines?
I always meet my deadline.

How do you value efficiency?
I am very efficient.

How do you organise your priorities?
I don't have a problem prioritising.

What is your favourite meal?
I think the food you cook here is great.

Interviewing the chef. For a chef's position, it is important to get a measure of the applicants' commitment to food. Try to be informal and build a dialogue with the candidate … *"I see that you've worked for … how was that?" "Tell me about your responsibilities? What style of food did they cook? What do you like to cook at home? What chefs do you admire? What restaurants do you like?"*

Tell them about the job and your expectation of how you see the successful applicant performing. Use the job analysis information or show the candidate the job description. Do not overload the applicant with information. By the latter part of the interview the candidate will have relaxed and may start being more expansive about their experience in the industry. You are looking for evidence to confirm your findings. With more discussion, you may feel that the candidate is an inappropriate choice. They may seem unable to want to change their habits and attitudes. Another candidate's response may make you feel that they are an excellent choice. The candidate however may need further training to become competent.

You need to consider the following questions. *How much training will be required? How long will this take? Can you wait? How much energy and commitment will be needed from you?*

General questions to consider. Below is a list to help in the evaluation of candidates during the interview.

Characteristics that you are evaluating *but not necessarily asking about.*
- What is the candidate's standard of efficiency?
- How would you rate the candidate's interpersonal skills?
- Does the candidate have the ability to do the job quickly but without losing quality?
- Does the candidate have the ability to juggle priorities that can change from one minute to the next?
- Does the candidate panic?
- Is the candidate methodical?
- Can the candidate get the job done in the priority that is most important right now?

Examples of questions that will offer an insight into the decision-making skills of a candidate.
- What sorts of problems, such as disputes or disagreements, have you encountered in a kitchen?
- How would you have dealt with the problem if you were in charge?
- Have you been in a situation where you suspected someone of stealing? How would you react?
- How do you train other staff? How important do you consider training?
- How do you design a menu? How do you cost it?
- How would you respond to a customer who has eaten a steak but then refused to pay for it because he said it was tough?
- How would you respond to a customer who is unhappy with his meal and starts to make a scene in the café?
- How would you manage the restaurant when you get swamped with customers?
- How would you respond to a staff member who refuses to do a task such as open bottles of wine at the table?
- How would you handle a waiter who regularly makes mistakes with customer's orders?

Remember that you drive the interview and if the candidate wants to chatter on, then you must control the direction. Wind it up when you are ready but with a statement that will explain to the candidate what to expect regarding a decision. *"We have had a lot of applicants and I hope to make a decision by next Friday. I will be in touch with you then when I may require you to come in for two evenings work experience"*.

OFFER OF JOB. It is important never to offer the job until you are sure that you have the right person. An offer can be legally binding. The offer is usually made by telephone. A letter confirming the appointment can follow or alternatively you can make a time for the candidate to come in and go through the offer. The offer should include a job description and employment contract. This becomes the first step of the induction process.

Induction. The induction process introduces a new employee to the culture of the organisation and helps them to feel part of the team. When an organisation has a large number of staff or a high turnover of staff, compiling an induction manual can save a lot of time. This may set out the organisation's philosophy, its vision and goals, as well as performance expectations for the staff. It may include basic training procedures and the rules of the organisation such as staff benefits, discounts on meals, weekly routines, holiday entitlements, etc. Some organisations will appoint a *mentor or buddy* to each new employee. The mentor works alongside the new person while they settle into the job. For a new employee they need to receive feedback during the first two months. Following this, an organisation should plan to have staff appraisals at least once a year. Every employee needs some form of appraisal.

EMPLOYMENT LAW: WARNING! If you do not want to end in the Employment Court with a personal grievance claim, you must understand the ramification of employment law. Before you start hiring staff, it is a sensible idea to attend a course or read a book on the subject. You will also find seminars run by the local Chamber of Commerce, Restaurant or Hotel Association or Polytechnic. The following discussion relates to procedures surrounding the Employment Contracts Act 1991 which is to be replaced by the Employment Relations Act. The body of case law that exists will still set legal precedents for resolving disputes.

Employment contracts have legal status and if things go wrong either party may cite breach of contract. Most problems arise in the area of dismissal for poor performance or serious misconduct. The employer's responsibility is to ensure that an employee has appropriate training and understands clearly what performance is required. Failure to perform to the appropriate level can be grounds for dismissal.

Summary dismissal is instant dismissal without notice. This is often the reaction of a manager who observes something serious such as theft or wilful damage. In order to minimise the risk of a personal grievance, a manager should avoid the temptation to dismiss on the spot. This can be a difficult request. The manager is angry, upset and provoked. It is precisely this reaction that often leads to a court case.

Constructive dismissal is when an employee leaves a job because the employer's behaviour has forced the employee to leave. It may be that the employer has made it impossible for the employee to do the job by publicly humiliating the person or withdrawing access to resources.

The Employment Court looks closely at procedural fairness. This means that if the employer has not followed the correct procedure, even if the employee was guilty, they can lose. The remedies offered under the Employment Contracts Act 1991 are reimbursement, reinstatement and compensation. For the employer, the worst case is to have dismissed an employee and then lose in court. The employee may ask to be reinstated in their job with compensation and the employer must pay both sets of legal fees. The whole exercise can cost thousands of dollars and result in needless hours of stress and worry.

Procedure for dismissal. If you have a problem with an employee and wish to dismiss them, it is important to take legal advice on the correct procedure. It is better to get the advice before you act to prevent costly mistakes.

1. *Verbal warning* to alert the employee to the problem.
2. *A written warning* often follows a verbal warning and formally states the problem and what is required to rectify it within a set time frame. The date must be reasonable (i.e. *by tomorrow* may be unreasonable). It should also state that failure to demonstrate an improvement may result in dismissal.
3. *Written notice of dismissal.* The employee is formally dismissed. The employee now has 90 working days to submit a notice of personal grievance to the employer.

---

1. Brillat-Savarin, *The Physiology of Taste*, 1970.

CHAPTER NINE

ACHIEVING THE STANDARD

A chieving the standard is about serving safe food and having competent, well-informed staff who understand the concept of quality. This chapter examines customer service, quality and communication and concludes with a section on food safety.

In Chapter Two we discussed the simple equation that underscores the success of a hospitality business.

> Good product + Good Service = Customer Satisfaction

People have become used to a more sophisticated level of dining. Customers are increasingly more discerning; they read magazines, travel regularly and enjoy eating a variety of cuisines. In recent years, the quality of food has improved considerably in New Zealand. The area of service delivery lags behind the standard of food produced in the kitchen. The key to good service is understanding how to build a relationship with your customers.

It was on that night that I realised what an orchestrational miracle it would one day be if we could ever figure out how to deliver the right food, at the right temperature, to the right person, at the right table, at the right time. I reasoned with myself that others before me had solved this mystery, but knew that we were a long way off.

Danny Meyer on opening night at Union Square Café in the Union Square Café Cookbook

BUILDING RELATIONSHIPS. People build relationships. The relationship between the buyer and the seller as they conduct a transaction is obvious. What is not so obvious is the dynamics that come into play during the transaction. The hospitality industry is special in that a relationship is often built the first time someone visits your café or restaurant. Staff and owners who recognise this are able to facilitate and speed up the relationship-creating process.

An article in the *Journal of Strategic Marketing*[1] defines a relationship as a *voluntary transaction based around mutual trust, commitment and reciprocity*. In a restaurant it is easy to see evidence of this. When a customer is greeted by a friendly, efficient staff member the relationship interaction commences. Trust is established but it is contingent on the meal or service delivering what it purports to do. Each can fulfil an unmet need in the other.

Relationships are dynamic and rely on the interactions of the partners to succeed. Underlying the relationship is always the need for both partners to feel reciprocal benefits. The customer wants to feel valued by the restaurant. Similarly, the restaurant wants to feel that the customer values their product. All too often, particularly in the hospitality industry, the reciprocity is unbalanced and one partner in the equation feels undervalued. When this happens that partner chooses to let the relationship fade and seeks out a more satisfactory substitute. It is not always the customer who feels undervalued. Restaurants and cafés who set up in small communities often feel distraught at the indifference shown to their business by the local people. Ironically it is often the people from outside the community who use their services more than the locals.

The issues about building a relationship are the same whether you own a bank, a service station or the supermarket. A customer who returns time after time needs to feel valued. It does not take much to engender this. The list below outlines what customers wish to experience.

Customers wish to experience:

1. **Recognition.** Smile. Even if you do not know their name, it is important to let the customer feel that you recognise and acknowledge them as a regular. The faster this happens, the quicker the customers will identify with you and support you.

2. **New ideas.** Regulars want **recommendations** about what to try. In doing this, the server is thinking about what the customer's preferences are.

3. **Happy staff.** When customers observe happy staff with a sense of humour, they feel more inclined to give of themselves. It draws one person to another.

4. A customer feels more confidence when the staff show **enthusiasm** and **energy** for the product, the organisation and the customer.

Successful real estate agents understand that before they even start to sell a house they must take time to get to know the client and build a relationship. Once they understand the client's expectations and build a sense of trust it is far easier to find the property that meets the client's needs. Supermarkets, on the other hand, struggle to build relationships with their customers. As a consequence, many customers have no sense of commitment to the supermarket and shop at different places depending on convenience and price. The supermarket staff, have no idea who is a good customer and who is not. For the customer, the supermarket bill can be their largest weekly expense and it is frustrating that this fact attaches little value. *"Do you know who I am? … I spend $300 here each week, which is $16,000 per year!"*

Encouraging the customer. The restaurant or café needs to encourage the customer to get to know the staff of the business. The customer should feel relaxed about talking with the staff and giving feedback. When the customer makes a reservation, they should discuss any special requirements. They can ask about the menu or specials and pick a wine so it can be ready to serve on arrival. When the staff know the customer they can personalise the service by allocating the best table or by doing something amazing, like baking a cake on a special occasion.

If customers are running late, they should call to let the restaurant know. If a customer books a table and then does not show up, they have breached their responsibility. At Hay's we will not hold the table after thirty minutes. When dining in large popular restaurants overseas, the diner often feels the pressure to eat and vacate the table for the next setting. Table-turn is an important efficiency ratio and if a restaurant can get two sittings every night their turnover and profit potential is increased. Busy restaurants should warn the customer when they book for 6.30 pm that the table will required for another booking at 8.30 pm.

Raising the Standard. *Benchmarking* is a concept that has been readily adopted by the hospitality industry. It enables businesses to measure their products and services with others. It is a form of competitor analysis but it also serves to raise the standard.

Much of the innovation in the hospitality industry has resulted from the experience of chefs and restaurateurs who have worked in quality restaurants or bars overseas. They have sought to achieve a similar standard in their own businesses when they have returned to New Zealand. Peter Thornley was Executive Chef at Blake's, a leading London hotel. Greg Heffernan spent five years in London, including a period at the Grand Metropolitan Hotel, before commencing as Executive Chef at Huka Lodge. This type of input has been the main impetus for the increase in the standards of the hospitality industry.

Restaurant reviews. Restaurants and cafés need reviews just as restaurant reviewers need them. Reviews give feedback and provide advice. The reviewer's comments do help to raise the general standard of the dining. Many reviewers are not professional writers or chefs and review from the point of view of one consumer to another. These reviews are mostly concerned with cost, value for money and service. Such reviewers are not interested or qualified to comment on technicalities. Any serious restaurant reviewer must spend time in a kitchen to understand the life of a dish, how it starts and is transformed. Reviews also *shine the spotlight* on hospitality businesses that are achieving excellence.

Competitions. For a new restaurant, café or bar, competitions can provide an excellent vehicle for getting established. They provide a set of criteria that challenges the business. For Hay's, the Corban's Wine and Food Challenge provided an annual focus as we strived to win the overall award. In setting this as our goal, we realised that to succeed we needed to reach a standard that was comparable to the best restaurants in town. By trying to achieve this, we in fact made the transition from café to restaurant. We identified the standard and as a consequence improved our own quality. The wine list and standard of service benefited directly from the attempt to achieve this goal.

What is Quality. Total Quality Management (TQM) was first established in Japan after World War II by a group of American advisors. It was rediscovered by American business during the 1980s! Quality is defined as the *goodness of the product as perceived by the customer*. Customer satisfaction is a synonym for quality. TQM focuses on improving the processes used to make a product or deliver a service. The cost of poor quality can be significant and often remains undetected unless people look for it. To do this the processes within a business must be analysed to understand where the quality problems may arise. Flow-charts, fish-bone diagrams, pareto charts and benchmarking are some of the tools used to identify the areas needing improvement. TQM is team based. It cannot be effective without the support of senior management and the participation of all staff members. The staff who deal with the customers receive their feedback and often know where the problems lie and what the best solutions would be. Quality objectives for a hospitality business could include the following:

- **Zero defects.** The goal is to have no defective products and to minimise the variability of a product. For example, the food served always reaches the standard. There is no variability in the dish when presented by different chefs. They all achieve the same standard.

- **Reduce the cost of poor quality and service.** When food is not cooked to the correct standard, it may have to be thrown out which results in wastage. The food may also need to be re-cooked, that is *reworked*. Reworking costs because the chef must spend time correcting the meal and new ingredients may have to be used. Reworking is inefficient.

- **Standardise** the level of service and quality by training all staff to the same standards.

- **Encourage teamwork,** responsibility and initiative. By encouraging staff to take responsibility, they will show initiative.

- **Achieve kaizen** which is defined as organised and continuous improvement. A motivated team will always find ways to improve the standard of product and service delivery.

- **Monitor the performance.** Obtain feedback by talking to customers, surveys and benchmarking your performance.

- **Establish long term relationships** with your suppliers and customers.

Who is the customer? TQM defines two types of customers. External customers are the obvious groupings such as the diner and the supplier. Internal customers are people within the organisation who depends on the actions of other members of the organisation. For example, the chef is the customer of the waiter. The waiter is the customer of the chef.

A flow-chart of a diner's interaction may be like this:

- Customer is greeted by the waiter.
  ↓
- Customer is seated.
  ↓
- Waiter recites today's specials and offers the wine list.
  ↓
- Waiter takes the order.
  ↓
- Waiter gives the order to the chef.
  ↓
- Chef cooks the meal.
  ↓
- Waiter takes the food to the customer.
  ↓
- Customer eats.
  ↓
- Customer pays the bill and leaves.

If an incorrect order is placed with the chef, then the process breaks down and the results are often disastrous.

- Customer tells the waiter the meal is not the right meal.
  ↓
- Waiter goes back to the kitchen and tells the chef.
  ↓
- Chef gets grumpy at the waiter for placing an incorrect order.
  ↓
- The first meal is thrown out.
  ↓
- A new meal is cooked.
  ↓
- Customer must wait twenty minutes for the meal to cook.
  ↓
- Customer refuses to pay because of the mistake.
  ↓
- Manager is called and insists that the customer pays.
  ↓
- The customer refuses to pay.
  ↓
- The customer vows never to return.
  ↓
- The customer tells all his friends about the experience.

Instead of the customer paying $20 for a main course, he has paid nothing. The restaurant has prepared two meals and made no money. The chef is grumpy because his resources and time have been wasted. The customer thinks that the restaurant is no good because the staff are incompetent.

> **TQM can be summarised in the The Deming Chain Reaction[2]**
> → Improve quality.
> → Decrease costs, less rework, fewer mistakes.
> → Improve productivity.
> → Decrease in prices results in increased market share.
> → Stay in business.
> → Provide jobs and more jobs.

THE CUSTOMER PROCEDURE. Good service involves standardising a procedure for service delivery. By establishing a series of quality checks, the example given above can be avoided. Below you will find an outline of the service delivery that we use at Hay's. This is the basis of our staff induction process.

1. **Greet and acknowledge.** Establish eye contact. If you are busy say, *"I won't be a minute"*.
2. **Use open body language.** Your sense of energy is evident by your posture. Relax. Have your shoulders back.
3. **Be confident.** Your confidence will make the diner feel confident that you know what you are doing. They will say *"Here is a professional"* and their expectations will be heightened.
4. **Discuss the menu.** If a customer asks for something that is not available then suggest alternatives. Offer a solution. Give the customer feedback. *"That's really delicious"*, *"That's a good choice"*.
5. **Repeat** the order back to confirm it to the customer.
6. **Discuss the wines.** *"Can I help you with your wine choice?" "Can I recommend a wine?"* The wine bottle is presented at the table and then opened.

> **Opening wine**
> • To open the bottle you need a quality wine knife and practice! Hold the bottle around the area above the label.
> • Smell the cork to check for cork taint (musty, dirty).
> • Wipe the opening of the bottle with a service cloth.
> • Let the person (sometimes referred to as the *host*) who has ordered the wine taste it.

- When this is confirmed, pour the wine. Return to fill the host's glass last.
- Fill the glass over the guest's right shoulder. Pour until ¾ of the glass is full or the approved level for the restaurant. Do not overfill.
- Once opened, white and red wine can be placed directly on the table.

Champagne/Mèthode
- Champagne should be opened by holding a service cloth over the *mussel* (wire around the cork) and twisting the bottom of the bottle.
- Once the guests have been served, the bottle should placed in an ice bucket.

7. **Serve the meal.** If possible serve from the left shoulder of the guest. Do not stretch in front of the guests. All meals should be brought to the table at once.

Quality check
To avoid customer disputes over quality, go back after two minutes to check and say *"Can I get you anything else?"* or *"How are your meals?"*

Going back when the diners have just started their meal enables the server to rectify any problems. *"I'd like some mustard."* *"The steak is too rare." "Where are the french fries?"*

It is these small issues that can become big issues if they are not dealt with at once.

If a customer is unhappy with the meal, it should be sent back to the kitchen. Customers should not eat the meal and then refuse to pay the bill.

8. **Clear the table.**
   Tables are cleared once all the diners have finished.
   - Take away from the right of the guest if possible.
   - Be consistent. Always take plates from the same side of each guest.
   - Do not stretch in front of the guests.
   - Do not stack the plates one on top of the other.
   - Take two or three plates at a time if possible.

9. **Prepare the bill.**
   There are two theories on preparing the bill.
   A) Wait for the customer to ask for the bill. This would be the normal procedure at more formal restaurants.
   B) Show that you anticipate the customers needs and do up the bill before they have to ask for it. Take it to the customer. At Hay's we do the latter because often the diners wish to eat quickly and leave. They appreciate not waiting around for the bill!

The three rules of good service
1. *Anticipate* the needs of the customer. Small things make big impressions so pay attention to detail.
2. Make the customer feel that this is *their space* for the evening.
3. *Under-promise and over-deliver.* Do not offer anything that you cannot deliver.

DEALING WITH A DISSATISFIED CUSTOMER. A customer's body language that will soon indicate if something is wrong. For example, they may avert their gaze when asked how the meal was, they may slump in their chair and look aggressive when the waiter comes near or the food is left untouched. The customer just wants the situation rectified. Summarised below is what leading service consultant, Michael LeBoeuf[3] writes about dissatisfied customers.

Dissatisfied customers
- 4% inform the business how they feel.
- 96% just go away.
- 91% of these customers will never come back.
- One customer tells 10 others of a bad experience.

---

1. **Listen** to what the customer has to say. Remain calm.
   Things to say include:
   - *"I'm glad you told me"*
   - *"Thank you for bringing it to my attention"*
   - *"I'm sorry"*
   - *"Let me try and help"*
2. **Accept responsibility.** Do not try to defend yourself or blame others. It is irrelevant. Avoid passing the buck; it only makes the problem bigger and takes longer to resolve. **Never argue** with the customer even if you believe they are wrong or mistaken. Arguing will only make matters worse.

3. **Offer a solution.** Deal with the problem. Take steps to correct it immediately and cheerfully. Never suggest an alternative that you cannot undertake.

   Check with your manager before you:
   • Offer them their money back.
   • Give them a complimentary *(comp)* item, such as a glass of wine or dessert or coffee.

COMMUNICATION. We live in an age of communication yet so often there is disagreement about the interpretation of what is being said by the sender and understood by the receiver. All relationships are built around understanding and being understood. What we say is not always what we mean. The non-verbal communication displayed by our bodies communicates much more than our words. For a manager and business owner learning how to read the body language of both your customers and employees is an essential skill.

How we communicate[4]
Non-verbal communication:
   eyes, face, body positions, gestures................................87%
Verbal communication: words.....................................9%
Other senses..4%

Most front of house people do not realise how they appear to customers. As they walk around the café, they are on show. Everyone is watching as they work and it is obvious whether someone is happy or grumpy. Below are some ideas on the interpretation of non-verbal communication.[5]

Facial expressions
• A smile means you are happy.
• A frown means you are sad, angry or irritable.

Arms
• Crossed arms mean that you are defensive or negative.
• Arm on your hips shows aggression or readiness.
• Arms on your head shows you feel dominant and superior.

Palm gestures
• An upward facing hand is submissive and non-threatening.
• Palms downward shows you are dominant and have authority.
• Palms closed to a fist and pointing a finger is aggressive.

Head position
- Nodding means affirmation.
- Head up indicates a neutral attitude to what you are hearing.
- Head tilt shows you are interested in what you are hearing.
- Head down shows you feel negative, bored or judgemental.

Eye contact
- To build a good relationship with another person your gaze should meet 60–70% of the time.
- Pupils dilate when people get excited.
- Closing your eyes while talking (*"talking down your nose"*) indicates superiority.

A gaze
- A business gaze should focus on the forehead.
- A social gaze focuses on the triangular area from eyes to nose.
- An intimate gaze focuses at parts of the person's body. This is inappropriate for business interactions.

Sitting position
- Being directly opposite is a competitive/defensive position.
- Being seated in a triangle position avoids direct body pointing and is less threatening.

Personal space
- **Intimate zone** (15–46 cm) indicates that you are emotionally close or alternatively that you are about to be attacked! Being too close makes people feel nervous.
- **Personal zone** (46 cm–1.2 m) is a social distance.
- **Social zone** (1.2–3.6 m) is a distance that strangers keep from each other.

> **Open body language consists of:**
> - Arms and legs apart.
> - Palms up and fingers loose.
> - Head is neutral or in a slightly tilted position.
> - A smile.
> - Eye contact.
> - A slight nod.

Habits to avoid
- Crouching beside a diner's table as this is an intrusion of their space.
- Standing too close to the table.
- Sitting down on a chair, unasked, to tell them about the menu. Again this is an invasion of their space.
- Having your feet and body pointing in the direction you want to go. This happens when you are in a rush and want to get to the next table. It indicates that you are anxious to leave.

INTERNATIONAL VISITORS. For international tourists, often their only experience of meeting local people is at their hotel or where they eat. Just sharing their news of what they did today means a lot to them. It does not matter if you ask all the customers the same questions. They will not know. The chances are they will never return to your establishment but they will recommend you to other travellers.

- *"Where did you come from today?"*
- *"What did you do today?"*
- *"Where are you off to tomorrow?"*
- *"How has your trip gone?"*
- *"What have you enjoyed most?"*

I will often go one step further and conduct some informal market research. I will often ask *"Where are you staying?"* so that I can track the different styles of accommodation our customers use. I will also ask *"How did you hear about us?"* This tells me about how our advertising is working and who is referring customers to us.

Non-English speakers. To communicate effectively with visitors that only understand a little English, you must speak slowly. New Zealanders tend to speak very fast and use a lot of slang, which makes it difficult for non-English speakers to comprehend. Try imagining how you would cope in a non-English speaking country. It is often simple sentences and single words that become the most effective method of communicating. In Japanese restaurants they often have photos or plastic *mock-ups* of the different meals with numbers. This is by far the easiest way to order!

In the hospitality industry, we try to be polite and therefore use words that we would not use in an everyday situation. The conditional tense asks *"Would you like to"*. Unfortunately people with limited English do not readily understand these words or tenses. Use simple sentences in the present tense and do not use too many words. By developing a familiarity with their words and using their jargon they will understand better.

It is very easy to confuse the visitor. Trying to describe all the ingredients in a dish can be confusing. Repeating an order back can be a traumatic experience, especially if you speak fast. The visitor will know the words for *fish*, *meat* and *dessert* but throw in all the descriptors that are used on a menu and they become confused. The most effective way is to simply state *"fish is salmon"*. When it comes to the order, say *"Fish – one, Lamb Rack – two, Chicken one"*. When it comes to payment, just print out the bill or write the amount on a piece of paper.

Turns of phrase

Difficult to understand	*Clear and precise*
How many people would you like to book for?	Your reservation? How many?
What can I get for you to drink this evening? Can I get you a drink from the bar?	Something to drink?
Our soup tonight is smoked mussel mussel broth with a coriander cream.	Soup is mussels.
Our fish tonight is seared tuna with an olive and anchovy crust.	Fish is tuna.
What would you like to order for dinner tonight?	Your order?
We cook the lamb medium rare.	Meat is pink.
Would you like a salad or a side order of shoestring fries?	Something else?
Is everything all right with your meal?	Meal OK?
Shall I get your bill now?	Check? Bill?

Coffee. People take their coffee in different ways.[6] When Europeans order an espresso, they mean a strong coffee served in a *demi-tasse* (half cup). A *shot* of coffee is around 30ml. In New Zealand we call an *espresso*, a strong coffee served in a cup of around 150ml, a *long black*. North Americans tend to ask for a *regular with sugar and cream* which means coffee that is not too strong, with sugar and milk on the side. A *flat white* is a single shot of coffee with velvety milk. A *caffe latte* is a double shot of coffee with a velvety milk and is traditionally served in a glass. A *cappuccino* is a single shot of coffee with foamy milk. A *caffe mocha* is a single shot of espresso blended with hot chocolate. A *ristretto* is a 15ml portion of espresso served in a demi-tasse. A *macchiato* is a single shot of espresso with a splash of milk.

FOOD SAFETY. This section briefly covers the most important aspects of food safety. It is recommended that you obtain and read other literature specialising in food safety, such as *Safe Food*,[7] by Pip Duncan and Liz Fitchett.

Food must be clean, safe and of good quality. Remember that quality is determined by what the ingredient is used for. For example, fresh unbruised bananas are required for serving in a fruit salad, while bruised over-ripe bananas make a delicious banana cake. Safe food will not contain food poisoning bacteria or other agents of food-borne disease. Poor food safety is very bad for your business and with serious incidents your business can be closed down. The reputation of the business can suffer as rumours about poor food safety get around. It also costs money because food may need to be thrown out and as a consequence the food cost percentage is not achieved.

The owner, manager and chef set the standard and therefore need to understand the rules for safe food and how they should be implemented. The first step is to ensure that the premises comply with the food hygiene regulations or have an audited Food Safety programme based on HACCP[8] procedures. The second step is to ensure that staff are trained so that they know how to comply with the standards. The rules should not be compromised even when a kitchen is busy.

In the home environment people also need to practice safe food. When a person suffers from food poisoning they are quick to blame the last meal that they purchased. However, sometimes this can be due to poor standards of hygiene in their own home.

Food spoilage. Food spoilage is the deterioration of food due to the growth of micro-organisms. Food spoilage may have some or all of the following characteristics:

- rotten smell or gas
- slime
- discolouration
- sourness

Micro-organisms include bacteria, yeasts, fungi, viruses, protozoa and other parasites. Micro-organisms are everywhere: in the air, in soil, in water, in food and on our hands. Spoiled food is not necessarily unsafe to eat.

Unless detailed laboratory tests are made, it is difficult to know whether food has been spoiled by harmless micro-organisms or by those that may cause illness in humans (pathogenic micro-organisms).

Food poisoning and other food-borne illnesses. Food poisoning is the most common type of food-borne illness. Food poisoning is generally understood to be illness which occurs as a result of consuming food contaminated by certain organisms or their toxins (e.g. salmonellosis, campylobacteriosis, toxin produced by *Staphylococcus sp.*), although strictly speaking it refers only to the illnesses caused by bacterial toxins in food. Other causes of food-borne illness are chemicals, metals, naturally occurring poisons, fungal toxins, algal toxins, viruses and parasites.

Bacteria. Bacteria are ubiquitous and the vast majority are absolutely harmless. In fact, some species of bacteria help us to make delicious cheeses and yoghurt, while others help to turn grass clippings into compost. Bacteria are invisible without the aid of a microscope. This means that they might be happily growing but you cannot see it happening. Occasionally bacteria will form *colonies* on food, in which case you can see them because millions of them group together. Bacteria can multiply fast given the right conditions (nutrients, warmth, moisture, time). Some bacteria can double in numbers every twenty minutes. In a practical sense, this means it is much worse to leave the pâté on the bench for an hour than it is to leave it there for ten minutes.

Anaerobic bacteria can grow without air, such as in jars or when vacuum-packed. Once vacuum-packed food is opened it should be taken out of its wrapping, covered and refrigerated. Vacuum-packed food should be consumed before the expiry date.

Staphylococcus aureus is a bacteria which can *infect* humans as well as make them vomit with its toxin. It is responsible for two different types of human illness. One type of infection is commonly seen as pustules or boils. Such boils are a hazard when present on food handlers. The other will result in severe vomiting and diarrhoea. *Staphylococcus aureus* and *Bacillus cereus* will grow in a variety of starchy foodstuffs (e.g. cooked rice, mashed potato) so long as adequate moisture is present.

Fungi. Fungi are also called moulds. A common one is the blue *Penicillium sp.* often found on old bread. Fungi do not often cause acute food-borne illness. However, the fungus *Aspergillus*, which may be found on mouldy nuts, can produce cancer-causing agents. Another dangerous fungus is the Deathcap Mushroom which contains very poisonous substances.

Spores. Some bacteria and fungi produce spores which can survive in soil for many years and are also resistant to heat. Food must be heated to 121°C (autoclave or pressure cooker) for 15 minutes in order to kill them. When conditions are right (nutrients, warmth, moisture, time), the spores *hatch* into normal bacteria or fungi. Examples of spore-forming food poisoning bacteria are *Clostridium botulinum* and *Bacillus cereus*.

Toxins. Some micro-organisms release *toxins* into food as they grow. Toxins may cause the person who eats the food to experience vomiting and diarrhoea, usually within 24 hours. Other toxins may have severe and long-lasting effects on other parts of the body, such as the nervous system. Some toxins are very heat resistant, so heating up affected food will not make it safe. This is why it is best to discard any food which may have had micro-organisms growing on it. Examples of bacteria that produce toxins are *Bacillus cereus* and *Staphylococcus aureus*.

Viruses. These cannot multiply in food so they must come from infected food handlers. Viral stomach illnesses (e.g. *Rotavirus, Norwalk agent*) are highly contagious. Often people with viral stomach illnesses are not so sick that they stay in bed. They then go to work while still contagious and infect others. Infected food handlers may shed large numbers of virus particles into the food and the person who eats the food may contract the virus. Hepatitis A is a virus which can also be contracted through eating contaminated food. The transmission of HIV and Hepatitis B usually requires the exchange of body fluids.

Other pathogenic micro-organisms. Diseases caused by protozoa and other parasites may be food-borne, although these organisms do not actually grow in food. *Giardia*, a protozoa, is usually contracted through contaminated water, though it can be passed on by infected food handlers. Untreated water should be boiled for three minutes to prevent *Giardia* poisoning. Parasitic diseases, such as hydatids and tapeworms, are often carried by animals. These organisms form cysts which survive for a long time in dry, dusty conditions.

Other types of poisoning. Naturally occurring poisons may be found in things like rhubarb leaves, some types of mushrooms, green potatoes and undercooked kidney beans. To remove the poisons from kidney beans, they should be soaked in water for two hours, rinsed and then boiled in fresh water until they are soft. Food handlers also need to be aware of poisoning by metals and other chemicals in the environment. Preventing such poisoning comes down to common sense.

- Wash all food.
- Store chemicals for cleaning and pest control away from food.
- Do not eat mushrooms unless you know they are safe.
- Do not use mercury thermometers in the kitchen.
- Do not store food in aluminium or cast iron cookware.
- Do not cook acid foods in aluminium or cast iron cookware.
- Remove food from tins once opened.

Below we will look at five steps that must be considered when planning your food safety programme.

1. Food storage

Food must be stored properly to minimise contamination by micro-organisms. Check the food when it is delivered to ensure it is of good quality. In a commercial kitchen all food should be covered and placed in containers off the floor. Make sure that animals are kept away from food storage, preparation and service areas. Cats and dogs are sources of *Campylobacter* and *Salmonella*.

In a refrigerator, raw meat should be covered and stored below cooked foods if they cannot be stored separately. If cooked food is to be used at a later time, it must be chilled quickly and then placed in a refrigerator. Putting hot food into a refrigerator will reduce its efficiency and slow down the rate of cooling. To cool food quickly, transfer it to small containers.

A microwave can be used to defrost food, but the food needs to be cooked immediately it is defrosted.

At-risk foods. At-risk or perishable foods are generally high in moisture. The risk of the foodstuff is increased if it is high in protein as well as moisture (e.g. egg custards, meat, milk). Acidic foods and those containing large amounts of sugar or salt are low risk.

High risk.......... Meats, fish, shellfish, eggs, milk, cream, stocks, sauces, cooked rice.

Low risk .... Foods with acids such as vinegar or lemon, sugar (jam, sweets), salt (salted peanuts, salami), fats and oils as well as dry or dehydrated food.

Chicken and poultry. Chicken spoils fast and is susceptible to contamination by a variety of bacteria, including those found in the bird's gut. Many live birds naturally carry micro-organisms, such as *Campylobacter* and *Salmonella* in their guts. These organisms can still be present on the chicken bought at the supermarket. It is particularly dangerous to eat poultry which is still bloody around the body cavity. This often occurs if the poultry is not properly defrosted before cooking. Poultry should be defrosted overnight in a refrigerator. It should not be left on a bench at room temperature nor be placed in warm water to thaw. Chicken should be heated to an internal temperature of 75–80°C during the cooking process.

Pork. Changes in the food safety standards of the pork industry have meant that pork can be served slightly pink rather than well-done as long as it reaches internal temperatures of 71–76°C during cooking.

Beef and lamb. Beef and lamb are two of the safest meats. In most instances they can be safely eaten rare. With large pieces of meat, it is only necessary to sear the outside. This is because any harmful organisms are normally found on the outside so the inside should be virtually sterile.

Fish. It is safe to eat fish raw as long as it is fresh. Japanese restaurants will always serve very fresh fish, but unless you have caught the fish yourself it is difficult to know precisely how fresh the fish is. Equal care must be taken with shellfish. Restaurants should always use a reputable seafood supplier.

Time-temperature abuse. Micro-organisms require nutrients, moisture, warmth and time in order to multiply. The growth of most bacteria is restricted at temperatures above 63°C and below 4°C. Temperatures between 4°C and 63°C are referred to as the **danger zone**. The danger can be controlled by minimising the length of time which *at-risk* foods are held in the danger zone. Food should not be left in the danger zone for more than two hours. Some bacteria and many fungi will slowly multiply below 4°C. Therefore two weeks' storage of a custard tart at 4°C is still time-temperature abuse even though the food was not in the danger zone. The temperature of refrigerators and coolers should be monitored to ensure that they are not above 4°C. Freezers should be set at –18°C.

Some organisms (e.g. *Yersinia enterocolitica*, *Bacillus cereus*, *Listeria monocytogenes*) can grow in a refrigerator and for this reason it pays not to refrigerate perishables, such as meat, cooked vegetables and custards, for more than a few days. Remember that the actual time will depend on the type of food being stored. All perishable food should be dated.

Cross-contamination. Cross-contamination is when micro-organisms from one product contaminate another product by way of a third party. An example would be if you cut salad vegetables on a chopping board where you had just cut up a raw chicken. Failing to wash your hands, the knife used and the chopping board could result in cross-contamination from the chicken to the vegetables. Dirty tea towels are also a source of cross-contamination.

2. Prevention of food spoilage

Food spoilage is prevented by inhibiting the organisms which cause it. Outlined below are some ways of doing this.

- **High levels of sugar or salt.** The addition of sugar or salt will prevent micro-organisms from growing. Preserves using sugar or brine are examples of this.

- **Reducing the pH level.** This is where the food is made more acidic, such as when vinegar is added to food. Micro-organisms are often used to do this, as in sauerkraut, wine and yoghurt production.

- **Drying.** Reducing the water content of foods will inhibit micro-organism growth. For example, a rich fruit cake is one of the most durable foodstuffs. Dried fruits and dried meat have a longer life than their fresh counterparts.

- **Heating and sealing.** Simply heating/cooking a foodstuff might extend its life, but to preserve the food you need to seal it so that micro-organisms cannot recolonise.

- **Cooling.** Refrigeration below 4°C slows down the growth of most micro-organisms.

- **Freezing.** Freezing can decrease the numbers of some organisms, but it will not kill them all. Once the food has defrosted the bacteria are free to multiply.

- **Preservatives.** Preservatives extend the life of a food by inhibiting the growth of micro-organisms. Preservatives include sodium metabisulphite, sodium benzoate, sodium citrate, sodium lactate and alcohol.

- **Antioxidants.** Antioxidants (e.g. ascorbic acid) do not inhibit the growth of micro-organisms, but they do stop the food from oxidising and developing unpleasant flavours.

3. Cleaning and sanitising

Cleaning and sanitising are an essential part of any food safety programme. A cleaning schedule ensures a systematic approach to cleaning using the appropriate cleaning materials. It should tell the reader what to clean, how often, the correct procedure and who is responsible.

- **Cleaning is usually done with detergent.** This removes visible contamination but it does not actually kill bacteria or any other micro-organisms. Contaminants, such as food residues or soil, can provide nutrients for bacteria and can also harbour their spores. Water from a tap should be heated to at least 60°C. Air-drying of dishes prevents cross-contamination from tea towels. It is important to ensure that the detergent is rinsed off.

- **Sanitising** kills micro-organisms. Dishwashers clean as well as sanitise. Sanitising units only sanitise. Dishwasher water should reach a temperature of at least 83°C. Sanitising includes spraying benches with methylated spirits or chemical sanitisers, as well as dipping cutlery or glasses in boiling water. There are a number of commercial sanitising products available. The surface must be clean before a sanitiser is used and this must be applied according to the manufacturer's instructions.

- **Sterilising** is an extreme form of sanitising. If something is sterile then it does not contain any living organisms. The only way to do this in the domestic kitchen is to use a pressure cooker. Some large commercial kitchens may have special sterilising equipment.

4. HACCP

Hazard Analysis of Critical Control Points (HACCP) is a written plan which describes how food should be prepared and served to ensure it is safe. If your business has a Food Safety Programme based on the principles of HACCP, which is approved and registered with the Ministry of Health, the business is then able to request an exemption from the food hygiene regulations. Regular audits of the business food safety practice are required.

HAZARD ANALYSIS OF CRITICAL CONTROL POINTS

Identifies points from delivery to service and manages systems to make food safe. HACCP involves identifying the hazards that influence food safety in the workplace, controlling and monitoring these hazards, and taking corrective action should the controls fail. It focuses on preventing the premises and its procedures from becoming unsafe in the first place.

Analyse hazards

There are three main types of hazard which cause food to become unsafe to eat.

1. **Intrinsic hazards** are hazardous by nature. For example, raw poultry, skin infections on food handlers which have not been dressed, vegetables with soil on them, rubbish bins and pest control poisons.
2. **Poor food handling hazards** occur when food becomes unsafe as a result of being in direct or indirect contact with an unsafe food or substance. This is called *cross-contamination*.
3. **Time-temperature abuse** is when food is kept between 4° and 63°C.

Control and monitor the hazards

Good food handling practices should prevent *cross-contamination*. Your food safety programme should include checks to make sure that the rules are followed. For example, who checks that the tea towels are washed regularly?

Take corrective action

When the controls have failed corrective action should take place. An example would be to throw out the custard tart stored for two weeks in the fridge or discard the tomato soup that was stored in an aluminium pot.

Rules for Safe Food.

1. Practise good personal hygiene.

- Wash your hands regularly, especially after you have been to the toilet. Clean your nails. Do not wear nail polish when working in the kitchen.
- Wear a clean uniform. Wear your hair up if it touches the collar. Wear a hat.
- Do not wear jewellery other than earring studs and a simple wedding band.
- Do not sneeze over food.
- Do not handle food with uncovered wounds.
- Do not touch pets without washing hands afterwards.

- Do not lick a spoon and then replace it in the food or taste food using your fingers.
- Do not come to work when you are sick.

2. Keep the kitchen clean.
- Implement regular cleaning. Dispose of rubbish regularly.
- Keep animals, rodents and insects out of the kitchen.
- Prevent cross-contamination.

3. Store food properly.
- Avoid time-temperature abuse.
- Minimise the length of time that food is between 4°C and 63°C.
- Appraise the food. An unpleasant smell or slimy appearance should be a warning that the food may be unsafe.

4. Cook food properly.
- Cook the food until it reaches the correct internal temperature.
- Follow the proper reheating procedure.

Occupational safety

There is very specific legislation covering safety in the workplace.
This ensures both employers and employees take responsibility and make every effort to identify and minimise hazards that staff may be exposed to. Some safety issues that are important for a hospitality business are outlined in the following box.

Common safety issues in a Kitchen
1. Lack of concentration while cooking can result in burns and cuts.
2. Avoid excessive haste in the kitchen.
3. Incorrect use of equipment can result in injury. In particular pay attention to knives, meat slicers, food processors and deep fryers.
4. Spills on the floor must be cleaned up immediately and a paper towel placed on top to warn others.
5. Deny access to all but kitchen staff.
6. Appropriate footwear must be worn at all times.

1. Gronhaug, K. et al. "Fading relationships in business markets." *Journal of Strategic Marketing*, Vol 7, Number 3, September 1999.
2. Walton, *The Deming Management Method*, 1989.
3. LeBoeuf, M. *How to win Customers and Keep them for Life.*
4. Fraser, K. *Interaction for Action*, 1994.
5. Pease, A. *Body Language*, 1981.
6. Allpress, *Barista Guide*, 1999.
7. Duncan, P. and Fitchett, L. *Safe Food*, 2nd ed. 1996.
8. Johnston, M., Shackelton, S., Duncan, P. *Safe and Sound*, 1994.

CHAPTER TEN

HOSPITALITY MARKETING

Marketing your business is the way to stay in business. Having the vision to build your business into a brand may become the most important element in creating a competitive advantage. This chapter discusses how to develop a marketing plan that will create an image and a presence in the marketplace. It assesses public relations and different types of advertising that can help build your brand.

In Chapter Three, we discussed the process of finding that *great idea* and discovered that in an over supplied market, *segmentation is the key*. The *great idea* was then evaluated in terms of the market and its competitors. Following this it is important to consider how to promote the business and set some marketing objectives.

- What is the *image* that you want to build?
- What is the *brand*?
- Where is the business *positioned* in the marketplace?
- Who are the *customers* that you wish to reach?
- How can you meet their *needs*?
- What is the marketing *budget*?

The pleasures of the table are peculiar to mankind and depend on preliminary care over the preparation of the meal, the choice of the place and the selection of the guests.

Brillat-Savarin in The Physiology of Taste

The marketing plan will formalise these objectives and the result should be a product with a distinct sense of identity or brand. Promotion is incremental and should never cease. As one campaign ends another one must start. Over time a series of small promotions results in raising the profile of the business. Most small businesses do not need to employ an advertising agency. Promoting a business need not be a costly exercise, all that is required is a little creativity to devise a cost-effective marketing plan.

Talk the talk. The manager or owner, in their role as *chief dispenser of enthusiasm,* must drive the marketing process and become the most energetic promoter of the business. The personal selling skills of everyone involved in the business will help spread the message and create converts. Everyone needs to be an advocate and *talk the talk,* including the chef hiding in the kitchen. Being seen at trade shows, seminars and meetings can open new opportunities and draw people to your business. Networking at such gatherings is a way of using your acquaintances to *spread the word* and influence how people view your product.

The preferences of consumers are often changed through becoming better informed. Olive oil is an ancient product yet in New Zealand the demand for olive oil only happened once consumers became aware of its health benefits and attributes as a cooking condiment. This demand was created through talking about olive oil at seminars, in newspapers and magazines. When Pedro first arrived in Christchurch in 1979 to set up his Spanish restaurant he had to purchase olive oil from the chemist! Some businesses cannot wait for word of mouth to work and this is where promotion becomes part of the package to raise their profile.

THE MARKETING PLAN. Marketers talk of the *marketing mix* which forms the basis of a marketing plan. It integrates the *4 P's of marketing.*[1] *Product* relates to the characteristics of the product such as the design or service offered. *Promotion* is how you communicate the product's ability to satisfy the customer's needs through sales staff, advertising, public relations and direct marketing. *Place* assesses the location and methods used to distribute the product and is often described as the *channels of distribution. Price* ensures that the product is priced at a level to maximise the sales and reflects a customer's perception of value.

A *marketing plan* details the promotional objectives to achieve the goals of the business. It does not need to be a complex analysis but should provide a simple action plan that summarises the marketing objectives for a period. Setting a promotional budget will determine the level of expenditure. Remember it is a good idea to set a generous budget as this will help you obtain your marketing goals faster.

For a new business a marketing plan needs to be determined well before the business opens. Once the business starts to trade the owner or manager often becomes preoccupied with operational issues. A marketing plan requires creative thinking and therefore mental space to come up with innovative ideas. The plan needs to be regularly updated. The time frame of the promotions should consider the time of year as the climate can impact on your selection of activities. Responsibilities should be delegated to ensure the plan and objectives are attained. The plan gives a framework and helps structure what you are doing.

For a hospitality business, developing relationships with customers can be the focus of a marketing plan. *Relationship marketing* focuses on attracting, maintaining and enhancing customer relationships.[2] This is the underlying premise of a hospitality business and much of the promotional activities planned should be centered on building relationships with customers. This in turn will help build a distinct identity for the business.

The list below demonstrates the type of promotions that a business may run in its first six months.

SAMPLE MARKETING PLAN
Month 1: Week 1
- *Soft* **opening.** This enables the business to standardise and fine-tune the quality of food and service.

- **Special function for strategic guests.** This can be organised for potential customers, suppliers and friends who will start the *word of mouth* process by recommending the business to others.

- **Press releases.** Specific media are targeted with stories informing them of the unique and beneficial product that you offer.

- **Printed leaflet.** A leaflet promoting the product can be distributed to the residents of the area where the business is located.

Week 3
- **Advertising supplement.** This appears in the local daily newspaper.

Month 2 Food section. A write-up about the chef, owner or business in the local newspaper's food section.

Month 3 Sponsor a community event. The local school or Lions Club is always looking for sponsorship which may take the form of a giveaway, such as a free meal for two.

Month 4 Wine tasting. This can be a promotion for customers in conjunction with a winery with whom you may form a strategic alliance.

Month 5 Regular ads. Small well-positioned ads in the newspaper publicising special events.

Month 6 Newsletter. The first newsletter is mailed to customers informing them of special events over the next 6–8 weeks. These events may include:
- A dinner for Valentine's Day or Mother's Day.
- A fashion parade for a local charity.
- Cooking demonstration.
- Special wine release.
- Arrival of Gisborne truffles.
- Arrival of porcini.
- Christmas promotion with specially priced set menus.

BUILDING RELATIONSHIPS.

Strategic people. For restaurants every diner is a potential restaurant reviewer because of their power to recommend or dissuade. Getting the business established can be helped by inviting strategic people who, through their network of friends and colleagues, can start the word of mouth process. Attendance at the opening launch or a special function can demonstrate that they support you and the product. A dinner invitation for a complimentary meal may be all that is needed to attract a well-known personality. A press release in the form of a personal letter may also entice them through the door. However, remember not to be too persistent! I was once pursued by a firm for over a year. They would ring me at work promoting their business. After several calls they offered to send a limousine to pick me up. The more they rang the more negative I became, until finally they rang me one evening at home. After that I lost complete interest in viewing their product. Given my own time I would have ventured forth to find them but the over-zealous representative alienated me.

Strategic alliances. These refer to building relationships with other businesses that may offer synergies. Complementary products can offer benefits to both sides and the obvious connection is with the beverage suppliers in the hospitality business. Beer, wine and spirit suppliers have far greater promotional budgets than an individual bar or café. They will often have ideas on how to promote your product and their product together. At Hay's we have an informal alliance with wineries such as Pegasus Bay and Daniel Schuster. They welcome our students to their winery and talk about wine production along with a tutored tasting of their wines. In turn we like to recommend their wine in our restaurant.

Community relations. Participation in community events is often a cost-effective way of becoming identified as part of a community. The school sports, the church fair and local service clubs may seem like a bottomless pit in their requests for resources but they do enable a business to introduce itself to new segments of the market. The more closely a business is identified with a community the more the community will support and claim it as its own. It is important to ensure that the community event that you are sponsoring is relevant to your industry or customer base and marketing plan. Sponsoring the local rugby club may be more appropriate for a sports bar than a café.

BUILDING A BRAND. Most hospitality businesses do not yet understand the importance of building and marketing a brand. A *brand* is often described as creating a distinct identity for a product or service. *Brand equity* is a phrase that is used to summarise the level of identification with the brand. A customer who buys the same brand of coffee year after year must like the product and therefore identifies with it. The more customers who feel this way about the brand of coffee, the greater the brand equity. In a competitive market, branding becomes the means to achieve *product differentiation*. When customers make a conscious choice to use your product over another because it is trusted and preferred, a competitive advantage is obtained.

Building a brand takes time and careful planning. Branding is just as important for a small delicatessen or coffee shop as it is for a large bar. Branding takes that *great idea* and turns it into a more valuable concept with its own identity. The brand often embodies the vision of the business. Successful branding will result in your product having more value in the marketplace.

Starbucks, the American coffee retailer, has extended the concept of a coffee bar to global brand. Coffee, mugs, T-shirts, coffee makers, ice cream and coffee milk drinks are all part of the products that it offers in its cafés and kiosks around the world. Gibbston Valley Winery near Queenstown offers a unique blend of premium wine producer and smart-casual dining with a tourist destination in the form of its wine cave. Built to cellar the wines in a controlled environment, the wine cave is now a tourist activity in its own right. The Gibbston brand is one of the leaders in the ascent of Central Otago as a rival of Burgundy.

Tony Astle and his wife Beth have established a brand for their restaurant. Nestled in a beautiful villa in Parnell, it features an exclusive Auckland dining experience. Tony has weathered many storms but still produces a product consistent with his vision. He has managed to stay at the top of the Auckland restaurant scene without dropping his standards or the quality of the experience. Over the years he has been criticised for the prices charged, but he has kept to his vision of offering the best. When people dine at Antoine's, they dine in the knowledge that this is a unique experience.

Julie Dalziel, the editor of *Cuisine* magazine, talked to *Her Business*[3] magazine about the need for *Cuisine* to broaden its readership and advertising base. Facing an onslaught of competition, as well as static demand for advertising space, *Cuisine* went out to build the brand. Through a carefully planned campaign they achieved their goals by advertising themselves. This heightened *Cuisine's* profile, increased their readership and improved their brand equity.

Logo. The first point of contact between a business and prospective customers will generally be its logo emblazoned on the signage or a promotional leaflet. The logo design can have an enormous impact on the business. A logo reinforces the image and also creates an impression. It gives credibility and inspires confidence. The logo is also the basis of many items used to promote the business, such as business cards, letterheads, flyers and of course signage.

An original and captivating design gives a personality to the business from the outset. For ideas, it is always instructive to examine logos of other successful businesses. Searching the pages of international magazines or websites can provide ideas on the sort of logo that you may wish to use. When it comes to the actual logo design, it is better to consult a graphic designer than attempt to do it yourself on a computer at home. A designer understands the use of fonts, style and colour which can enhance the image. This process does take time. Hasty decisions can often result in a poor choice.

Signage. Successful businesses recognise the significance of signage to growing the business. Just like the logo, a sign is critical to creating an impression and drawing people into the business. The signage is working for a business twenty-four hours every day, seven days a week. Neon and other illuminated signs can be very expensive but they are visible day and night. A sign-written awning may be just as effective. Sandwich boards work well in conjunction with other signage. They are cheap to make and can enhance your presence on a busy street. It has become a fashion for some cafés to use blackboards with provocative messages to capture the wandering eye of a driver pausing at an intersection.

NEW IS NEWS. When a business is new, it is news and must proactively seek free editorial in the media. Even if the business is not new you can create news, such as special events to punctuate the year. Inspired by Chez Panisse we began an annual Garlic Dinner which has a set menu matched with wines. Theme evenings such as *Sherlock Holmes' Revenge* or Fondue parties also capture the imagination of tireless foodies. Other events can include cooking classes, wine tastings and seminars. When the café wins a competition, this is news and should be promoted.

Press release. To receive free editorial, a press release must be written to tell the news aspect or to illustrate an interesting angle. The copy of a well-written press release can often be used directly in a publication. It is important to find out who is the best person to send the press release to as the busy editor may just throw it in the rubbish tin. A telephone call to the organisation may provide this information.

To write a press release you must develop an engaging style of writing that captures the attention of the reader who in many cases will be the food editor or a reporter. The first two sentences are the most important ones. They must be punchy and arresting and tell the reader the main information that you wish to convey. When starting to write a press release it may help to practise saying out loud what you wish to communicate. Interview yourself. What are you doing? Why is it of interest? What is different or unique? When is it happening?

If you do not feel comfortable writing about your business, contract a public relations (PR) consultant. A PR consultant is experienced at discovering *newsworthy* stories to share about your business. They understand the way the media works and how to increase the profile of the business.

It is always a good idea to include a photograph taken professionally to accompany the press release. It strengthens the story and the publication may use it alongside the story.

> **Some tips for writing effective press releases**
> - Maximum length: two pages, with a line spacing of one and a half.
> - Use emboldened headings for each topic.
> - Pretend you are a journalist and use short sentences.
> - Make one point in each sentence. Be concise.
> - Avoid using the first person (I think, I like, we found).
> - Avoid using colloquialisms unless in italics *"a place frequented by beautiful people"*.
> - Avoid personal bias or opinions.
> - Proof-read what you have written, checking for grammar and spelling. Have a break then re-read what you have written.
> - Get someone else to check what you have written.
> - Enclose contact details so they can call you back.
> - Enclose a photograph taken professionally to accompany the story.

FREE MEDIA EXPOSURE. A marketing plan can be based around achieving as much free publicity as possible. Most large daily papers in New Zealand have a food section that runs on a specific day of the week. If you are doing something new and interesting then they will be happy to hear from you. A personal call to the food editor to follow up on the press release can be a good idea. Local community newspapers may be interested from a local news aspect.

It is a mistake to send the same press release to every publication. There must be an element of exclusivity. If you send the same story and they all run the same copy, next time the publication may not print anything for fear that their competitors will be running an identical story. Food editors wish to appear impartial and not to seem to favour one organisation over another. They may run the story this month but pass up a subsequent story in two months' time.

It is better to create two or three different stories which are directly targeted to the segments that the newspaper or magazine focuses on. These can be placed over a period with different publications. An innovative fit-out will be of interest to the publications that specialise in design. *Cuisine* features "newsy snippets" in the magazine's front section as well as in the page entitled *Lady Lunchalot*. *House & Garden* is interested in news but will cover it in the format of an article written by one its writers. *Hospitality Magazine* may also give you coverage, as may the food sections in *North and South*, the *Listener*, *Next* and the *Women's Weekly* to name but a few.

Radio and television. Radio interviews offer another opportunity to use free media exposure to target potential customers. National Radio may set up an interview in one of its food slots. Talk-back is another avenue but again there must be an element of news. Often air-time is linked to advertising. Some stations will accept a promotion, such as a free meal giveaway, while others insist that it is part of a larger advertising campaign.

Local television channels have created a demand for more local content. Chances are that if you are opening a café this will not be of sufficient news interest to feature on a channel's news or lifestyle programme. That is, unless you do something extraordinary, such as mount your collection of hub-caps on the wall of the café or offer snails raised in your garden!

PROMOTIONAL MATERIAL. When a business first opens it is very useful to have promotional material, such as business cards and leaflets, ready to hand out to happy customers and to prospect for new ones. Preparing a leaflet takes time and planning and there is probably a three to four week wait between concept and delivery. While photocopying is inexpensive and easy, photocopies on cheap coloured paper may not have much impact nor reinforce the image that you wish to create. For large quantities of printing or cards it is more cost-effective to use a printer. In recent years the cost of colour printing has dropped considerably. Always obtain several quotes to get a feel for the cost.

Printed letterheads and business cards. The quality of paper used for letterheads is always important in reinforcing the image. In the past, heavy laid papers gave an aura of respectability and quality; today these papers are too heavy to be used in a laser printer. The result can be a great letterhead with an illegible laser-printed message. It never ceases to amaze me how many business cards I use. At Hay's we have them placed on the counter and each week the stock is replenished. Customers take them because they wish to recall the experience or stay in touch. A business card is a simple but effective way of communication.

DIRECT MARKETING. This refers to the promotions that are targeted directly at the customer, reaching them at their home or office by telephone, mail or the internet. Flyers and catalogues through the post and telemarketing of special promotions are widely used tools with a strong *call to action*. Spreadsheets have made compiling mailing lists of customers a simple exercise. In North America online booking and point of sales systems enable restaurants to track their customers as well as analyse their purchases. Restaurants can develop a comprehensive list of a customer's preferences. In New Zealand, the Privacy Act prevents you from compiling a mailing list without the person's permission and anyone can request to be removed.

Newsletter. A regular newsletter is an excellent way of keeping in touch. A graphic designer can create an attractive newsletter format that will support the image of the business. Newsletters need to be regular to be effective. A quarterly or biannual newsletter should hold the interest of your customers. Too often and the newsletter will lose impact. A newsletter can contain news about special promotions. It should also include a *call to action* designed to stimulate a response by offering a competition or promotional giveaway. You may wish to devise a frequent diner reward system where regular patronage is recognised with a free meal or bottle of wine.

Distribution. Distribution of promotional leaflets or letters can pose problems. You can do it yourself if you can justify the time. Your friends or children may also offer to help but they will probably get bored after the first three hours. New Zealand Post offers distribution services through contractors who can distribute the leaflet with the other *junk mail* or with the *posties*. There are price differences between the two. For maximum effect it is better to pay the premium and opt for the postie, as your fabulous flyer is more likely reach the hands of the prospective customer. This service enables you to specify the exact street addresses that you wish to target. You are able to segment by street, suburb or even postal box. If you start to develop a mailing list it is possible to cut the distribution costs by sorting the mail according to the postal areas and then taking it to the bulk mail counter at NZ Post. Sorting will drop the cost of postage from 40c to 28c per letter for every thousand letters sent.

Distribution can also be done by fax or the internet. Fax works best if you know who will be receiving the leaflet and if they are not worried about the poor copy reproduction or the flimsy thermal paper that is used by so many faxes. Faxes often lack impact and are very easy to throw in the rubbish. Collecting e-mail addresses for prospective customers can be difficult and time consuming but in the future this will become a popular means of communicating, especially as food lends itself to the interactive medium of the internet.

PAID ADVERTISING. There will come a point when you just have to accept the fact that it is necessary to pay for advertising. While Anita Roddick and Dick Hubbard tell us they spend very little on advertising, most of us know that without some help the brand will languish. Advertising does cost, but with careful planning it should increase sales and brand awareness.

There are countless ways to advertise your product. The mix of advertising that you choose should be targeted at the desired market segments. A two-week promotional campaign using radio ads backed up with a series of newspaper ads and a direct mail drop will penetrate a number of market segments. Radio and television *(broadcast media)* are used for immediate response and are ideal for promotions such as sales or special offers. Consumers are enticed with simple messages such as *"Call now"*. Print media advertising can carry much more information than broadcast advertising. Large ads with editorial about the product can read like an article and be very successful. So too can full colour ads that feature a good photo with minimal words as they can create an image far more powerful than a page of words.

Ratings rule. Advertising charges are driven by circulation and market share. While the big daily newspapers are published every day except Sunday, there can be huge variations in the circulation between the Friday and Saturday issues. All media has their circulation and market share audited. If you watch television it is often quite easy to tell when this is about to happen as radio stations and newspapers often run promotions just prior to an audit. The greater the market share that a radio or television channel has, the more it can charge for advertising.

The advertising executive. If I place an ad in a paper, such as *The Press* or the *Sunday Star Times*, in response to this I will receive phone calls and e-mails from advertising executives around New Zealand prospecting for my advertising dollar. I suppose this demonstrates initiative on their behalf. For inexperienced advertisers however, the choice of where to advertise can be confusing especially when faced with a persuasive advertising executive. It is helpful if you already have in place a marketing plan as this will help you make up your mind. Do not feel that you have to make an instant decision. I usually ask a series of questions.

Ask the advertising executive:
1. Who is the publication's target market? (Age, gender, income of readership)
2. What is the distribution/circulation?
3. What is the cost of the ad? If you divide the cost by the circulation, you should get a good comparison of cost from one publication to another.
4. Send me a sample of the style of publication with the advertising rates.

It is important to get quotes on advertising campaigns and to ask if they have special deals or free editorial. At certain times of the year there may be rate reductions or incentives. When it comes to making a decision you must feel free to say *"No, that is not my target market"*. A persistent executive will challenge this and want to convince you otherwise. My reply to this is *"Thank you for your concern but I have made my decision"* or alternatively *"I have already determined my marketing budget and this has been allocated"*.

Newspaper advertising. Newspapers contain news today and old news tomorrow. Ads in newspapers must be placed in good positions to create impact. When advertising I prefer to opt for a loading where the placement of the advertisement is guaranteed. This is a more expensive option. When I advertise in *The Press*, our local Christchurch paper, my preferred spot is page three. The front page is too costly but, in general, most people will always look at page three; following that they look at page two. After this the readership of the paper becomes dispersed. The TV page and increasingly the food section are also good positions. To get on page three however, I must book a year in advance!

Advertising supplements are another option. This is paid *advertorial* where you receive editorial promoting your product. This can vary in size from half a page to a double page spread. The price can be subsidised by advertisements from suppliers who are happy to support the business by taking an advertisement. Supplements create impact because they can feature a number of stories and pictures of the business in a large format.

Magazine advertising. In recent years there has been a proliferation of glossy magazine titles. Some have a greater following than others and it is worth checking their circulation figures before making a commitment. Magazines such as *Cuisine* and *House & Garden* have a far greater longevity than a newspaper but the advertising can cost more. Their subscribers treasure the issues and they often end up on the coffee table for friends to enjoy. Cafés, doctors' or dentists' waiting rooms, office reception areas and staff cafeterias seem to collect old issues. The position of the ad is important. Securing a spot on the right-hand page toward the front of the magazine is preferable.

Radio advertising. Radio advertising has become so segmented that unless you advertise regularly it is difficult to assess its effectiveness. Years ago everyone knew which station to advertise with but today there are so many options. Prime-time radio ads on a premium station can cost over $200 for a 30-second ad. One ad will not achieve much, so to run a week-long campaign can cost a minimum of $3000. The local Polytechnic may ring you with a cheap ad campaign on their campus station but this may not target the segment you wish to attract.

Some businesses find radio a very successful medium but it can depend on what you are promoting. Saturation advertising occurs when a lot of ads are run to drive home the message. The Warehouse understands the power of saturation and they would not keep doing it if they did not find it effective.

Television advertising. There are two standards of television advertising: the local community stations and the networks. Channels like TV One have regular regional breakouts that are less expensive than ads run nationally. They only appear in the designated region. The local community channels are in a similar situation to the radio stations in that a profusion of channels has resulted in a loss of brand identity. Viewers surf the channels often not knowing which channel they are watching. Car yards and retailers find ads on local channels can achieve a good response. Some hospitality businesses, particularly family restaurants, run successful local television campaigns. With television there is the added expense of filming an advertisement.

Television advertising needs to be regularly updated to maintain impact. It is only exceptional ads that can withstand the test of time. After a period, most appear dated and tired.

THE INTERNET. The internet is a force that is beginning to pervade our lives. It is very easy to design and set up a website. This can cost under $2000. What is difficult is attracting regular visitors to the site. Each month more and more sites come online so there is a lot of competition. Ironically to ensure that a website works effectively you must be prepared to advertise it. Establishing *hyperlinks* with other websites is a good start but this requires several hours each week just monitoring what is going on and e-mailing other sites to organise a link.

We have a website for Hay's and the School of Food and Wine called http://www.foodandwine.co.nz. It is listed in an American directory of cooking schools so we get many inquires from that source. I am always intrigued when I go to the site usage statistics to see who has been visiting and the pages they have looked at. I used a young computer designer to set up the site and he encouraged me to have a page called *"Celia's recipe of the month"*. I was a bit dubious about the benefits of this but curiously it is the second most visited page on the website! Our website works well because we are constantly advertising our courses. If the site was only for the restaurant I doubt that we could justify our own site. It would be better to be part of a bigger directory and linked to some key dining or tourism sites.

A website must be current. It is often dated on the home page. When surfing the net, I do feel pleased when I find sites that are recently updated. It makes me feel that they are current and therefore relevant. While we have our menu and wine list on the website and regularly update it, we still make changes to the menu that do not appear on the website. It is somewhat disconcerting to have diners arrive with their printed out copy of the menu and wine list to find that their carefully chosen selection has been removed!

ADS THAT WORK. Marketers tell us that we only see what we are looking for. If you wish to buy a car you will suddenly see all the ads for cars. Once you have bought the car, you will not be so interested in car advertisements. On a Friday night a customer may wish to go out for a meal and search through the newspaper or the yellow pages to find a place. During the rest of the week, the customer will not be interested in places advertising food.

Call to action. Successful advertisements should include a *call to action*. This results in the prospective customer being inspired to respond to the ad, *Now!* The following statements are all designed to stimulate a response.

Buy this and win a dinner for two . . .
Enter now and go into a draw . . .
Come on Monday night and be eligible to win . . .
The offer finishes tonight!

Simple messages. With any advertising it is important to have a clear understanding of what you are trying to say. This is your *vision* for the ad. The key is to have a simple uncomplicated message. When writing the copy for an ad it is always tempting to incorporate as much information as you can fit in the space. A cluttered ad full of words and diverse images is very difficult to comprehend. At Hay's, in our advertising we use the phrase *Eat Lamb* alongside a glossy photo. It is very basic but effectively conveys the message even when the reader does not speak a lot of English.

Creating an emotional response. Effective ads, particularly those on television, are successful because they produce an emotional response in people. *Music* creates a mood or atmosphere. *Humour* gives rise to familiarity although humour is hard to convey in hospitality advertising without resorting to a Basil Fawlty satire. This may not be the sort of image that you wish to foster!

Use of certain words also prompts a reaction. In an era when people often have high incomes but not enough time to enjoy their prosperity, *ease* and *convenience* can be key motivators. *Lifestyle, leisure* and *pleasure* underly many consumer decisions. Eating in a café or restaurant is a choice that balances the need to eat with the pleasure that the process gives.

Some people are motivated by *nostalgia* for things past. This is particularly true for food; *"It tastes just like the pie that Granny Bea used to make . . . ".* Old well-tried recipes have the respectability of time and hark back to a golden era when life was less complicated. They are often simple, honest statements of goodness.

As people age they become more preoccupied with issues of health and personal well-being. The debate on genetically modified food has aroused an interest from consumers for information about what they are eating. Serving organic food offers an interesting marketing opportunity for hospitality businesses.

The customer wants to feel happy about their purchase. Toyota understands this. This is why for years they have run generic ads, not necessarily selling a particular car but selling the *"Toyota way"* and the *feel-good* that the ads manage to engender. The ads affirm that you made the right decision; that you are proud to be associated with the company. *Cognitive dissonance* is when you feel negative thoughts after purchasing a product. *"I wish I hadn't bought it." "It's not the same as the one I tried in the shop."*

ADDITIONAL SALES. The diner's table offers opportunities for promotion.
A diner will always look at *the table talker* (a leaflet or tent card placed on
the table) just because there may be nothing else to do while they wait to be
served. This material may promote a special meal, special event or a specific
wine that may be featured as the *wine of the month*. Blackboards, posters and
static displays of bottles of wine are all methods of promotion. The staff
are an essential element in this marketing mix for they are able to make
recommendations to the customer. Often a promotion will be backed up
with a system of rewards for waiting staff. They may gain a bonus in the
form of a product when they reach a certain target. Large liquor companies
also offer a host of branded merchandise to promote a campaign. It is
common to see T-shirts, aprons, wine buckets and umbrellas to subliminally
promote a product.

Successful cafés, restaurant and bars will sometimes offer their own
branded merchandise for sale such as T-shirts, hats, preserves and postcards.
These provide additional sales income but also help promote the business
elsewhere. The merchandise becomes a personal endorsement by
the purchaser.

ADDITIONAL SALES PROMOTIONS

- **Table-talkers** offer information about promotions and special
  events but should not overly clutter the table.
- **Window displays** and **bar displays** can effectively promote
  special products.
- **Sandwich boards** and **blackboards** within the premises or on
  the footpath can be used to feature the promotion.
- **Tags** are floppy items attached to a product, such as the neck
  of a wine bottle. They are effective at catching your eye because
  such a tag is not normally there.
- **Posters** that attractively promote a product are positioned
  around the premises, such as on walls, pillars or in the
  toilet area.
- **Promotional ice buckets, aprons, umbrellas, banners and
  signage** can also be used to advertise certain products.

TRACKING YOUR PERFORMANCE. When you advertise or promote a
product it is always important to evaluate the response. As discussed in
Chapter Three surveys are a common method of evaluating performance.
Getting feedback from customers and suppliers about the effectiveness of
a campaign can be beneficial.

Ads which include a call to action contain built-in feedback. When you offer a coupon or a prize, you should be able to directly observe the level of response. Many ads however are focused on building brand recognition rather than a call to action so that when you start thinking of buying a car, you will immediately think of Toyota. I will always ask people how they heard about us. For many of our students at the School of Food and Wine, it has taken them years to actually call up and enrol. But somewhere the connection has been made and they have stored the information for future reference. Tracking the performance of your ads can be a frustrating exercise!

Non-Customers. For any business it is important to understand who are the *non-customers*, that is those people that do not use your product or service. The *non-customers* of a hospitality business can be very obvious. They are the people who choose to dine elsewhere or drink next door. For some reason your business does not meet their needs and there can be numerous reasons for this. It may be they do not like the location or the ambience and are just happy dining elsewhere. The *non-customers* present market segments yet to be conquered and therefore can offer new opportunities for growth.

1. Assael, H. *Principles of Marketing* 1993.
2. Reid, R *Hospitality Marketing Management*, 1989.
3. *Her Business*, May-June 1998.

CHAPTER ELEVEN

SO YOU MADE IT

To stay ahead, that is to maintain a competitive advantage, you must innovate, refresh and re-invent your product. This chapter discusses strategies for renewal. Renewal is as important on a personal level as it is for a business

Fortunately for the hospitality industry, its products of food and beverage are necessities of life. They do not become obsolete like computers or cell phones. As people cook less at home they need somewhere to eat. Given the situation where a business has nurtured the products and the customers, and the economic conditions are favourable, demand should go on indefinitely. The future prospects are bright.

In this industry the key factor behind staying in business, besides the external economic pressures, is the commitment of the owner. The owner must still believe in the vision. For this to happen, the owner must feel enthusiastic and resolute in making the business work. Customers discern whether a business is thriving or not. To create an impression of success the business needs to demonstrate confidence and pride in what it does.

No matter what the industry, we think the true measure of service is the level of honest hospitality and value being offered. How well people feel treated will always be the determining factor in whether they come back for more.

Danny Meyer, *in* Union Square Café Cookbook

A business is dynamic. It is vital, moving, changing and evolving. It was a revelation to me, early in my business life, to discover this phenomenon. Once I recognised that change and evolution were inevitable and essential, I stopped trying to get to the point where everything was completed and there was nothing else to do. I realised that while I was still focused on making the business better, that point would continually elude me. There was always some new challenge.

Change is inevitable. Change creates new opportunities and they are everywhere if you open your eyes. Look out. Look ahead. Read. Keep informed. Listen to your customers. You will learn far more from your customers about your product than you can from a business consultant. Talk with your competitors. Benchmark the business.

PERSONAL RENEWAL. If an owner is tired, grumpy and short-tempered with the customers and staff there are two options. The first is to go on holiday and reinvigorate oneself; the second is to sell. Ignoring both options will result in declining sales. We have discussed in Chapter Six the importance of personal development to achieve a sense of personal renewal. It can be a very simple task. For instance, I find living in Pigeon Bay has given me the best of both worlds: the city, with the business, its responsibilities and stimulation, and the farm, looking north over the omnipresent sea, to Kaikoura. I can step back from the business, by sitting on our verandah and contemplating the movement of the wind on the water and the sun receding below the skyline.

Working hard. It is salutary to remember that you do not need to work all the time to be doing a good job. Business owners often think that they are trapped in the prison of their business. They feel that they are working 70 hours each week, although in reality it is often only 48 hours. There is never a complete break when they stop thinking about the business.

It is always easier to measure the time spent doing a task than it is to measure the actual results. Some owners find it difficult to delegate and to objectively evaluate the situation. It is hard to estimate the benefits of just taking a break. Going to Australia or California or eating at someone else's bar or restaurant, can be the stimulant that is needed.

BUSINESS RENEWAL. In Chapter Three we talked of setting goals. For a business to renew itself, it must retain a sense of direction and a deep understanding of what it is and where it is headed. Conducting a simple S.W.O.T. analysis will throw up ideas for consideration in your strategy. The planning process helps to elucidate the opportunities and provides a means to manage change.

In conducting an appraisal, whether of an individual or a business, it is important to reflect on what have you achieved so far; the path you have travelled. Recognition of this is always restorative. Enjoy your achievements as well as your plans.

Strategic planning is also about attempting to predict the future by anticipating trends. In this way the business can be seen to be looking ahead. Often a competitive advantage will be protected only by the ability to anticipate change. Deciding to change something can take courage.[1] A change of direction may not seem obvious or inevitable until the change has been implemented. It will then seem as if it was just a natural progression.

Arrogance and complacency. Arrogance and complacency are two of the products of success. A bar that is *pulling all the noters*, the important people in town, feels important itself. The restaurant that has won every award can also fall into this trap. Self-importance is an insidious vice and should be discouraged. A self-important business will never be an innovator because it becomes too preoccupied with its current status to look to the future. There is always room for improvement of your product and the service. There are always new niches to attract.

Attracting the *non-customers*. Renewal can be driven by focusing on those people who do not use your services. These are new segments of the market. Ironically it is trying to attract the non-customers that may lead to more innovation. But, paradoxically, often when the business seeks to attract the non-customers, it alienates the existing loyal ones.

The market. If the business is experiencing a decline in sales, it is important to evaluate the reasons for this. *Is it a temporary aberration? Is there still demand from the market segments?* Look to your competitors and consider how they are doing. For the hospitality industry, the economic climate and the number of tourists can be a significant factor in determining demand.

BUSINESS STRATEGIES. A business can employ a number of strategies as it seeks to determine its future path.
- **Growth strategies.** Once the owner has decided to keep involved in the business, a growth strategy must be implemented to turn the business around and make it profitable again. Essentially this involves revisiting the great ideas of Chapter Three. The owner must look to new ideas, new market segments and products that will stimulate growth. For a hospitality business this can include a re-fit of the restaurant or café where the décor is refreshed and the image refocused.

- **Profit strategies.** This strategy focuses on maximising the competitive advantage of the business. The business uses existing resources to focus on profit. The objective may be to sell the business in the future.

- **A milk or harvest strategy.** This strategy aims to generate sufficient cash without having to spend any more money. The withdrawn resources may be invested elsewhere. This strategy creates a holding environment while the owner may make a decision on whether to sell the business or reinvest and improve it.

- **Sell.** This strategy is when the decision is made to sell the business as a going concern. To achieve the best sale price it is important to have the accounts showing a sound profit. If the accounts do not demonstrate that the business is desirable it will not sell well.

- **Liquidate.** This strategy enables the assets of the business to be sold and therefore generate some income. This process can be managed as the business is wound down and inventories reduced with the intention of closing down completely.

Which to choose? Selling the business has its own set of problems. Not the least is finding someone to buy the business. Often an owner will decide, two years before they want to sell, to pursue a profit strategy where they focus all their energy on building the business so that it looks attractive to a prospective purchaser. To do this the owner must still spend money on advertising and maintain the premises. When you *milk* a business, you avoid spending money but sometimes this results in a decline in sales and it can be counter-productive. A decline in sales will indicate to a purchaser that the business is not what it once was.

Stephanie Alexander tried to sell her landmark Melbourne business for several years without success. The strong identification of the business with her made it very difficult to sell. This was Stephanie's, a Melbourne icon. It was a fine-dining restaurant in a market that preferred noisy bistros. For a person to buy the business they would constantly face the comparisons with its previous owner. One night in 1998 when she was in Italy, she decided to liquidate. Liquidation meant selling all the fixtures and fittings at a discount. It also meant redundancy payments for her staff. After Stephanie announced her intention to close, the restaurant traded frantically until New Year's Eve 1998 when it closed forever.

Refit the business. Refitting does not have to involve a glamorous refurbishment. When you have spent a lot of money on a fit-out, the cost of changing it can be considerable. Special fittings, such as expensive paintings that were trend-setters when the business first opened, now look dated. But what do you do with them? Custom-made fittings have often very little salvage value. They are a **sunk cost**.

A new colour scheme which enlivens the décor may be effective. Often a hospitality refit includes a new image for the business with new uniforms, a new logo, new awnings and new signage. It gives the customers a sense that the business is evolving, as long as you do not negate the positive aspects of the image you have already created.

Vinnies, an Auckland icon, has during ten years of hard work established itself as a leading restaurant offering inspiring food with refreshing combinations of ingredients. Snuggled unobtrusively in two old shops in Jervois Road, it is easy to miss. A refit has given it new ambience and energy. The private dining room lined with ponga and ferns gives a distinctly New Zealand atmosphere in a restaurant offering a unique dining experience.

Why businesses fail. Businesses fail for a variety of reasons. Failure to understand that the business needs to renew itself is common. Below is a list of other causes.

- **Overcapitalised.** Too much money has been spent on set-up of the business and the owner is not receiving a return on their investment.

- **Undercapitalised.** Most businesses are undercapitalised and do not have sufficient reserves to expand in the way that they intend.

- **External Factors.** The internal economy and the economies of those countries who send many tourists (Japan, Australia, USA, UK, etc) to New Zealand can have an effect on the profitability of a business.

- **Marketing.** Lack of a marketing plan to reinforce where the business intends to go. Lack of market research.

- **Leadership.** Lack of vision for renewal. This may occur with an autocratic leader who is resistant to change and has lost interest in the business.

- **Management.** Cannot inspire the staff and customers.

- **Lack of innovation** or willingness to change.

- **Location.** Inappropriate location, for example, a difficult place to get to or poor signage.

- **Financial Controls.** Poor costings or no costings so that the profit is not achieved. Staff theft of product or money.

- **Big Projects**. While often a project is a good idea, sometimes these do not work and drag the business under.

- **Competition.** There is too much competition and the business fails to create a competitive advantage.

FOUNDATIONS OF SUCCESS. Over the previous chapters, I have discussed a range of issues that are part of making a hospitality business successful. Many are very obvious and therefore easy to implement. The challenge is to translate the theoretical issues covered in this book into reality. The result will be successful hospitality businesses that are valued by their customers, their staff and above all their owners. Below are some of the important factors that I think make up a successful hospitality business. Good Luck!

Foundations for success
1. Develop a **great idea** (product/service).
2. **Segment** the market.
3. Understand the market especially your **competitors**.
4. Find a good **location**. Be Accessible!
5. Have sufficient **finance** to establish and grow the business.
6. Know your **costs** and what you need to charge to make a profit.
7. Build a **team** to support you and your idea.
8. Establish a relationship with your **customers**.
9. **Market** what you do and create converts.
10. Allow **time** to become established and build relationships.

B I B L I O G R A P H Y

1. Aaker, David A, *Strategic Market Management*, 4th Edition, John Wiley and Sons, USA, Canada, 1995
2. Allpress, M *Barista Guide*, Allpress Espresso, Auckland, 1999
3. Assael, H *Marketing Principles and Strategy* 2nd, Dryden Press, Fort Worth, 1993
4. Bertolli, Paul with Waters, Alice *Chez Panisse Cooking*, Random House, New York, 1988
5. Boaz, Alyse *Marketing in New Zealand 2nd Ed*, Addison,Wesley, Longman, Auckland, 1999
6. Brandt, S *Entrepreneuring: The Ten Commandments for Building a Growth Company*, Penguin, USA, 1982
7. Brillat-Savarin *The Physiology of Taste*, Penguin UK, 1970
8. Coltman, M *Hospitality Management Accounting* 6th Ed, John Wiley and Sons, New York, 1998
9. Connellan, Thomas K *Inside the Magic Kingdom, Seven Keys to Disney Success*, Bard Press, USA, 1996
10. Covey, Stephen R *The 7 Habits of Highly Effective People*, Simon and Schuster, USA, 1989
11. David, Elizabeth *French Provincial Cooking*, Penguin, UK, 1960
12. Dornenburg, A and Page, K *Dining Out*, John Wiley and Sons, New York, 1998
13. Drucker, P F *Management Challenges for the 21st Century*, Harper Collins, USA, 1999
14. Drucker, P F *Adventures of a Bystander*, Wiley and Sons, USA, 1994
15. Dryden, G and Vos, J, *The Learning Revolution*, The Learning Web/ Bateman, NZ, 1997
16. Duncan, P and Fitchett, L *Safe Food*, (2nd Ed), Addison, Wesley Longman, Auckland, 1996
17. Fisher, R and Ury, W *Getting to Yes*, 2nd Ed, Arrow Books, London, 1991
18. Flandrin, J and Montanari, M *Food: A Culinary History*, Colombia University Press, New York, 1999
19. Fraser, K and Anderson, B *Interaction for Action*, Longman Paul, Auckland, 1994 *Harvard Managementor*, Harvard Business School, USA, 1998
20. Hawken, Paul *Growing a Business*, Simon and Schuster, New York, 1987
21. Hamilton, R and English, J *The Small Business Book*, Bridget Williams, Wellington, 1997
22. Henderson, B *The Logic of Business Strategy*, Ballinger Publishing, Boston, 1984
23. Hubbard, J; Thomas, C and Varnham, S *Principles of Law for New Zealand Business*, Addison Wesley Longman, Auckland, 1999
24. Jacobs, Lauraine *Cuisine Restaurant Guide, Auckland 2000*, Cuisine Publications, Auckland, 1999
25. *Journal of Strategic Marketing*, USA, Vol 7, Number 3 September 1999. Gronhaug, Kjeli *et al.* "Fading relationships in business markets". S Ratneshwar, S *et al.* "Product, person and purpose: putting the consumer back in to the theories of dynamic market behaviour".
26. Kawasaki, G *Rules for Revolutionaries*, Harper Collins, USA, 1999
27. *Larousse Gastronomique*, Reed, UK, 1990
28. Lewis, Morkel, and Hubbard, *Australian Strategic Management*, Prentice Hall, Australia, 1993
29. Hospitality Standards Institute *A Certificate in Wine Handbook*, Wellington, 1997
30. Meyer, D and Romano, M *The Union Square Café Cookbook*, Harper Collins, New York, 1994
31. Millar, S & Dreyer, W *Managing Human Resources in New Zealand*, Longman, Auckland, 1997
32. Millar, S *Managing Organisations in New Zealand*, Pearson Education Ltd, Auckland, 1999
33. Millon, M and K *The Food Lover's Companion to France*, Little, Brown and Co, London, 1996

34. Moore, G *Crossing the Chasm*, Harper Business, USA, 1991

35. Montana Wines Ltd, Montana Wine College, *Marlborough Wine Course Manual*

36. *Organisational Dynamics*, A quarterly review of organisational behaviour for professional managers, Briscoe, J and Hall, D *"Grooming and Picking – Leaders using competency frameworks"*, American Management Association, Autumn, 1999

37. Oster, Sharon *Modern Contemporary Analysis*, 3rd Ed, Oxford University Press, New York, 1999

38. Parken, Michael *Economics*, Addison, Wesley, USA, 1990

39. Pavesic, David *Fundamental Principles of Restaurant Cost Control*, Prentice Hall, New Jersey, 1998

40. Pease, Allan *Body Language*, Camel Publishing, Australia, 1981

41. Peters, Tom *The Pursuit of WOW!* Vintage Original, California, 1994

42. Peters, Tom *The Circle of Innovation*, Alfred A Knopf, USA, 1997

43. Rasmussen, E and Lamm, F *An Introduction to Employment Relations in New Zealand*, Addison, Wesley, Longman, Auckland, 1999

44. Reardon, Joan *Celebrating the Pleasures of the Table*, Harmony, New York, 1994

45. Reid, Robert *Hospitality Marketing Management*, 2nd Ed, John Wiley, USA, 1989

46. Robb, Alan J *Dictionary of Accounting and Finance Terms*, 4th Ed, Addison, Wesley, Longman, Auckland, 1996

47. Rudman, R *Human Resources Management in New Zealand*, 2nd Ed, Longman, 1997

48. Roddick, Anita *Body and Soul*, Ebury Press, London, 1991

49. Schultz, H and Yang, D *Pour Your Heart Into It*, Hyperion, New York, 1997

50. Walton, M *The Deming Management Method*, W H Allen, London, 1989

Costing a Menu

At the School of Food and Wine, we recommend to students that when costing a dish they should factor in a margin for wastage. A costing formula may includes a 5% or 10% margin for wastage. The reason for this is that, given the list of variables that come into play, achieving the desired food ratio is extremely difficult.

Using a Calculator

For some people, it has been a long time since you were confronted with a calculator. When costing food it is important to remember the power of the decimal point. On a calculator 0.5 is the same as half and can equal 500g which is half a kilogram.

On the calculator

1	=	1.0	=	1000g	=	1 kilo
.5	=	0.500	=	500g		
.05	=	0.050	=	50g		
.005	=	0.005	=	5g		

To calculate the cost of 150g taken from a 450g packet costing $7 per packet, you must do the following 150g/450g = 33%; 7 x .33 = $2.31

Bacon and eggs for 4

Ingredients	Quantity	Price per kilo	Subtotal	Total
Eggs	8	$2.40 per dozen		
Bacon	300g	$9.50		
Toast	8 slices	1 pkt has 18 slices and costs $2.20		
Butter	30g	500g costs $2.80		
Tomato	100g	$5.40		
Parsley	20g	$16.50		
			x 3 x1.125 *Retail price ÷ 4*	

Meatballs for 4

Ingredients	Quantity	Price per kilo	Subtotal	Total
Burghul wheat	85g	$2.65		
Mince	225g	$5.80		
Coriander	25g	$22.50		
Onion	150g	$1.80		
Garlic	5g	$10.80		
Soy sauce	20mls	1 bottle of soy (350mls) costs $2.90		
Tomato paste	35g	1 jar (450g) costs $1.95		
Pepper	incidental			
Oil	20mls	$14.30		
			x 3 x 1.125 *Retail price ÷ 4*	

Gougere for 4

Ingredients	Quantity	Price per kilo	Subtotal	Total
Flour	105g	$1.25		
Cayenne	pinch			
Butter	85g			
Water	220mls			
Eggs	3			
Cheese	55g	$11.40		
Parmesan	15g	$28.50		

Filling

Ingredients	Quantity	Price per kilo	Subtotal	Total
Chicken breast	340g	$10.60		
Onion	150g			
Mushroom	300g	$14.50		
Cream	80mls	300mls costs $2.10		
Tarragon	5g	$24.50		
Stock	290mls	400mls costs $2.89		
			x 3 x 1.125 *Retail Price ÷ 4*	

The following are indicative prices and are only meant as a guide to help you with the initial budgets.

Costs for setting up Restaurant/Café with a bar – 50 seats

Qty		Unit cost	Cost	Sub total
	Inside Seating			
15	Square tables seating 2	$400	$6,000	
3	Tables seating 6	$600	$1,800	
40	Chairs	$150	$6,000	
	Banquette: seating 10		$1,500	$15,300
	Outside Seating			
4	Tables seating 4	$250	$1,000	
20	Chairs	$100	$2,000	
5	Umbrellas with your logo	$300	$1,500	
	Paving		$1,500	$6,000
	Restaurant			
	Nice things on the walls		$5,000	
	Sound system		$1,500	
	CDs to play		$500	
	Planter boxes		$500	
	Menu folders		$500	
	Lighting: dimmers, halogens		$1,000	
	Carpet, flooring		$3,000	
	Painting		$2,000	$14,000
	Bar			
2	3m Formica bench, Melamine shelves, glass rack, sink		$5,000	
	Bar fridge		$6,000	
	Cash register		$2,000	$13,000
	Takeaway counter			
	3m Formica bench, Melamine shelves		$2,500	
	EFTPOS terminal cost		$1,500	
	Refrigerated food cabinet		$5,000	
	Cash register		$2,000	$11,000
	Coffee			
	Coffee machine		$6,000	
	Coffee grinder		$1,000	
	Zip hot water heater		$800	
	Shakers (chocolate, cinnamon), jugs		$50	
	Plumbing of coffee machine		$500	
	Coffee counter joinery and shelves		$1,500	$9,350

Qty		Unit cost	Cost	Sub total
	Coffee crockery			
6	Porcelain tea pots	$25	$150	
6	Milk jugs	$5	$30	
20	Espresso cups	$4	$80	
20	Cappuccino cups	$4	$80	
60	Saucers	$2	$120	
5	Demi-tasse	$4	$20	
20	Latte	$5	$100	
10	Sugar bowls	$5	$50	
20	Salt/pepper shakers	$15	$300	
2	Pepper grinders	$60	$120	$1,050
	Cutlery			
60	Large knives	$2	$120	
60	Large forks	$2	$120	
60	Small knives	$2	$120	
60	Small forks	$2	$120	
60	Dessert spoons	$2	$120	
30	Soup spoons	$2	$60	
50	Teaspoons	$1	$50	
20	Steak knives	$2	$60	
20	Cake forks	$1	$20	
1	Cutlery rack	$15	$15	$805
	Glasses			
15	Spirit pourers	$10	$150	
1	Vacu-Vin & stoppers		$100	
2	Wine knives	$15	$30	
60	150ml wine glasses	$3	$180	
40	Champagne glasses	$3	$120	
40	Beer glasses	$3	$120	
30	Shot glasses	$2	$60	
20	Spirit glasses	$2	$40	
60	Water glasses	$2	$120	
12	Water jugs	$10	$120	$1,040
	Crockery			
40	Large main-sized plates	$16	$640	
20	Large main-sized bowl plates	$16	$320	
30	Soup bowls (double as salad bowls)	$12	$360	
30	Side plates	$7	$210	
30	Small main/dessert plates	$8	$240	
20	Medium ramekins	$2	$40	
30	Small ramekins (optional)	$2	$45	
20	Deep salad bowls (optional)	$5	$100	$1,955
	Heater		$300	
	Vacuum cleaner		$500	$800

Qty		Unit cost	Cost	Sub total
Operational necessities				
	Reservations book/diary		$25	
	Calculator		$5	
20	Docket books	$8	$150	
1	Invoice book		$25	
	EFTPOS/till rolls		$150	
	Paper serviettes		$100	
	Security system		$800	
	Safe		$400	
2	Fire extinguishers		$600	
	Fax machine/answer phone		$1,000	$81,705
	Kitchen fit-out			
	Services			
	Painting costs		$2,000	
	Phone connection, 2 lines		$200	
	Power connection		$500	
	Plumber condenser drains, grease trap, sinks, hot water cylinder		$3,000	
	Gas installation (2 x 3 minimum)		$1,200	
	Lino flooring, coved		$1,500	$8,400
	Kitchen			
	Thermowave oven		$1,600	
6	Gas hobs		$4,000	
	Salamander		$1,800	
	Microwave		$400	
	Extraction system		$5,000	
	Deep fryer		$500	$13,300
	Kitchen joinery			
2	3m Stainless steel kitchen units/benches		$4,000	
4	3m high Dry store Melamine shelving		$2,000	
	Dishwasher area stainless benches		$1,500	
	Handwashing sink		$200	
	Produce/vegetable washing sink		$1,000	
2	Large dishwashing sinks		$500	$9,200
	Refrigeration			
	Walk-in chiller with shelving		$15,000	
2	Small service fridges		$800	
	Freezer		$1,500	$17,300

Qty		Unit cost	Cost	Sub total
	Lighting			
4	Heat lamps & space 6 plates		$1,000	
12	Power points		$500	
	Electrician		$2,000	$3,500
	Pizza/Bread			
	Pizza oven		$7,000	
	Dough mixer		$4,000	$11,000
	Dishwashing			
	Dishwasher/steriliser		$4,000	
2	Plate trays for dishwasher	$30	$60	
2	Flat trays for dishwasher	$30	$60	
1	Wine rack for dishwasher	$30	$30	
1	Champagne rack for dishwasher	$30	$30	$4,180
	Kitchen equipment			
	Food processor	$500	$500	
	Kenwood	$450	$450	
	Electronic scales	$500	$500	
	Spice grinder (optional)	$65	$65	
	Toaster (optional)	$60	$60	
	Ice-cream machine (optional)	$800	$800	
	Meat slicer (optional)	$800	$800	
3	Kitchen stools	$60	$180	
	Electric hand-beater (optional)	$35	$35	$3,390
	Baking equipment			
3	Large baking trays	$15	$45	
2	Medium baking trays	$12	$24	
6	Deep baking tins	$12	$72	
2	12 cup muffin tins	$12	$24	
2	Large cake tins	$12	$24	
2	Large flan tins with loose bottom	$12	$24	
10	Baskets for bread	$2	$20	
1	Rolling pin	$25	$25	$258
	Storage containers			
10	4 litre plastic containers	$2	$20	
3	20 litre buckers (flour/sugar)	$15	$45	
3	10 litre buckets for storage	$15	$45	
4	Medium meat trays	$12	$48	
2	Large bins	$12	$24	
6	1 litre containers	$1	$6	
2	Plastic pottles	$35	$70	$258

Qty		Unit cost	Cost	Sub total
	Pots			
2	Large stock pots	$150	$300	
2	Medium large pots	$65	$130	
4	Medium small pots	$55	$220	
3	Small pots or metal jugs	$45	$135	
8	Pizza pans	$10	$80	
4	Spiders	$10	$40	
1	Storage rack for utensils	$15	$15	
4	Roasting pans (optional)	$25	$100	
4	Large cast iron pans	$30	$120	
2	Medium pans	$20	$40	
2	Large woks (optional)	$20	$40	
3	Large chopping boards (meat, fish, veg)	$35	$105	
1	Small chopping board (slicing meat)	$15	$15	$1,400
	Utensils			
7	Assorted sized ladles	$6	$42	
6	Assorted wooden spoons	$1	$6	
2	Spatulas	$6	$12	
2	Balloon whisks	$15	$30	
2	Pallet knifes	$20	$40	
1	Bread knife	$60	$60	
1	Fish boning knife	$60	$60	
1	Meat boning knife	$60	$60	
2	8" Cook's knives	$85	$170	
2	Paring knives	$60	$120	
2	Small serated knives	$6	$12	
2	Potato peelers	$2	$4	
1	Can opener	$6	$6	
6	Meat hooks	$1	$6	
2	Graters	$3	$6	
2	Piping bags with nozzles	$10	$20	
1	Potato masher	$15	$15	
1	Fish slice	$3	$3	
1	Bench scraper	$3	$3	
2	Slotted spoons	$3	$3	
2	Large kitchen spoons	$2	$4	
1	Kitchen clock	$5	$5	
3	Tongs	$2	$6	
3	Cake racks	$6	$18	
1	Pizza cutter (optional)	$9	$9	
2	Pastry brushes	$2	$4	
1	Pair kitchen scissors	$15	$15	
1	Large steel	$25	$25	
1	Sharpening stone	$25	$25	$724
	Bowls			
6	Large metal bowls	$6	$36	
4	Medium metal bowls	$6	$24	
6	Small metal bowls	$5	$30	
6	Assorted plastic bowls	$4	$24	$114

Qty		Unit cost	Cost	Sub total
	Miscellaneous			
3	Cake tins (storage)	$15	$45	
1	Basic stationery (pens, paper, tape, stapler, etc.)	$15	$15	
1	Fire blanket	$35	$35	
1	First aid kit	$70	$70	
2	Gas gun/matches	$15	$30	
1	Notice board/clipboard	$100	$100	
1	Large conical sieve	$75	$75	
2	Sieves	$6	$12	
	Large roll tinfoil		$40	
1	Vegetable strainer	$6	$6	
1	Large metal colander	$15	$15	
2	Medium metal colanders	$15	$40	
1	Mandolin (optional)	$120	$120	
3	Rolls non-stick baking paper	$6	$18	$661
1	Large roll plastic film		$40	$73,685
	Cleaning setup			
6	Plugs	$2	$12	
2	Rubbish bins	$45	$90	
1	Kitchen broom	$15	$15	
1	Mop	$15	$15	
1	Bucket	$25	$25	
1	Brush/shovel	$5	$5	
1	Rubbish bags	$40	$40	
1	Degreaser/oven cleaner	$140	$140	
1	Cloths	$20	$20	
1	Box surgical gloves	$62	$62	
4	Pairs gloves	$2	$8	
2	Paper towels	$2	$4	
6	Stainless steel pads	$2	$12	
1	4 litre bleach	$30	$30	
1	5 litre detergent	$25	$25	
1	20 litre sterilising liquid	$140	$140	
2	Dishwasher brushes	$5	$10	
1	5 litre Handy Andy	$35	$35	
12	Aprons	$15	$180	
50	Tea towels	$1	$50	
2	2 pkts Handy towels	$2	$4	
1	Multi spray	$4	$4	
1	Cleaning cupboard – with sink	$500	$500	$1,418
	Toilets			
	Toilets – urinal, paraplegic		$2,000	
	Joinery		$1,500	
2	Hand dryers	$350	$600	$4,100

Qty	Unit cost	Cost	Sub total
Laundry			
Washing machine		$1,200	
Dryer		$500	$1,700
Operating set up			
Legal set up cost, company, lease		$2,000	
Insurance		$3,000	
Accountant		$2,000	
Architect		$2,000	
Licences: Environmental		$500	
Sale of Liquor		$1,000	
Resource consents/building consent		$1,500	
Letterhead paper		$400	
Business cards		$200	$12,600
Inventory Stock			
Food		$6,000	
Liquor		$6,000	$12,000
Administration			
Computer		$3,000	
Accounting/wages software		$1,000	$4,000
Signage			
Neon/illuminated signage		$5,000	
Awning		$1,000	
Specials boards, etc.		$500	$6,500
Start up advertising			$10,000
Summary			
Front of house		$81,705	
Kitchen		$73,685	
Cleaning Equipment		$3,118	
Operating		$12,600	
Stock		$12,000	
Administration		$4,000	
Signage		$6,500	
Advertising		$10,000	$203,608
Less landlord		$26,150	
		$177,458	

Qty	Unit cost	Cost	Sub total
Landlord fitout: Negotiable with your landlord?			
Legal costs for lease		$1,500	
Flooring, lino, carpets		$5,000	
Toilets to Environmental Health standard		$1,500	
Plumbing: grease trap		$500	
Electrical: upgrade, lights, connect		$1,000	
Telephone: system, connection		$200	
Power		$450	
Painting of walls		$4,000	
Building repairs, upgrade		$2,000	
Garden landscape			
Rent holiday			
Air conditioning		$5,000	
Extraction fan		$5,000	$26,150

INDEX

A

Aaker, David, 28, 38
Accounting information, 60
Accounting ratios, 63, 64
Achieving the standard, 121
Advertisement, for staff, 113
Advertising executive, 153
Advertising, 143–148
   expenses, 62
   free media, 150
   internet, 155
   paid advertising, 152–156
   writing, 113
Airey, Mavis, 32
Akaroa Bakery, 43
Alexander, Stephanie, 162
Appraisals, 99, 119, 160
Assistant chef, responsibilities, 110
Astle, Tony, 147

B

Bacteria, 135–140
Bardellis, 70
Bar, 10, 12, 25, 31, 37, 42, 43, 45, 62, 66, 72,
   88, 89, 98, 124, 161
   café-bar experience, 20
   food cost, 77
   gross profit, 62
   merchandise, 157
   security, 106
   set-up costs, 66
Beverages, costing, 88
Blackboard menu, 82
Bluff oysters, 71
Body language, 48, 99, 101, 102, 116, 127,
   129, 130, 131
Boston Consulting Group, 74
Brand
   building, 19, 143, 147, 148, 152, 154, 158
   loyalty, 35
Brandt's ten commandments, 67
Brandt, Steven, 67
Brasserie Flipp, 31
Brigittes, 33
Brillat-Savarin, 11, 16, 69, 108, 143
Business Life Cycle, 22, 23, 24, 25
Business Plan, 27

C

Café, 9, 10, 12, 25, 31, 32, 33, 34, 35, 43, 44,
   45, 64, 70, 79, 81, 83, 147
   experience, 20
   fixed costs, 76
   food costs, 77
   relationships, 122
   security, 106
   set-up costs, 66
   sales, 157
Carême, 11
Chef, employing, 107–112
Chez Eelco, 43
Chez Panisse, 15, 81, 82, 83, 88, 148
Christchurch Casino, 36, 44, 49
Cloudy Bay Wines, 42
Coffee, types, 12, 20, 32, 133, 134
Cognitive dissonance, 156
Commerce Act 1986, 57
Communication, 101, 121, 130, 151
Companies Act 1993, 54, 57
Competitor analysis, 27, 40, 47, 124
Constructive dismissal, 120
Consumer Guarantees Act 1993, 58
Contracts, 56, 119
Contribution margin, 62, 70, 74, 75, 88
Cost structure, 21, 41, 69, 76
Costing, food, 73–80
   beverages, 88
Covey, Stephen, 30, 95
Coyotes, 31, 45
Cross contamination, 139–142
Cuisine Magazine, 25, 148, 150, 154
Curnonsky, 11
Customer procedure, 127
Customers, 16, 23, 25, 26, 27, 32, 33, 34,
   39, 41, 42, 48, 64, 72, 77, 78, 81, 88, 103,
   107, 109, 111, 112, 114, 118, 121, 147
   analysis, 38
   confidence, 97
   count, 65
   dissatisfied, 129
   encouraging, 123
   expectations, 69, 70, 83, 122
   external, 125
   listen, 160
   non-customers, 158, 161

procedure, 127
quality check, 128
relationships, 145
segment, 35, 37
survey, 51

D
Dalziel, Julie, 148
Demand, law of, 43, 44
Direct marketing, 151, 152
Dismissal, procedure, 120
Disney, 98
Dissatisfied customer, 129
Drucker, Peter, 93, 98
Dux de Lux, 98

E
Employing, 103–120
Employment Contracts Act 1991, 10, 119, 120
Employment law, 59, 109, 119
Environmental analysis, 40
Equal Pay Act 1972, 60
Equation of satisfaction, 22, 24, 121
Escoffier, 11
Espresso *124*, 45
Experience curve, 80

F
Failure, business, 163
Fair Trading Act 1986, 57
Feedback, 51, 95, 98, 105, 116, 119, 123, 124, 125, 127, 157, 158
negative, 99
Financial accounting, 61
Fixed costs, 62, 74, 75, 76
Flash points, 111
Food cost percentage, 63, 73, 74, 75, 76, 77, 79
Food safety, 134–142
Food spoilage, 134, 139
Franchise, 34, 41
French cuisine, 11
Front of House, responsibilities, 104–108
Fusion cuisine, 13

G
Gibbston Valley Winery, 147
Goals, 27–31, 81, 93, 95, 97, 99, 119, 144, 148, 160
Good service, rules of, 129
Gourmand scale, 108
Great idea, 29–46, 143, 161
Gross profit percentage, 62, 63, 70, 73, 74, 76, 77, 89, 106
Growth/share analysis, 74

H
HACCP, Hazard Analysis of Critical Control Points, 134, 141
Hay's, 31, 32, 37, 38, 42, 43, 44, 46, 51, 65, 83, 86, 87, 88, 104, 105, 123, 124, 127, 129, 146, 151, 155, 156
Health and Safety in Employment Act 1992, 59, 106, 142
Heffernan, Greg, 124
Holidays Act 1981, 60
Hospitality Business Life Cycle, 22, 23, 24
Hospitality ratios, 63, 64
Host, being a, 15–28
Huka Lodge, 33, 124
Human Rights Act 1993, 59, 113
Hunter, Jane, 33

I
Income Tax Act 1994, 60
International visitors, 105, 132, 133
Interview, 49, 104, 113–120

J
Jacobs, Lauraine, 25, 103
Job analysis, 114
Jolly Poacher, 44, 45

K
KFC, 34, 41

L
L'Affare, 34
La Varenne, 11
Leading questions, 49
Leadership, 93–102
chef as leader, 108
styles, 94, 95
Legal structure, 27, 53, 54, 55
Logo, 18, 148, 163

M

McCormack, John, 45
McDonald's, 34, 82
Management accounting, 60
Manager, employing, 9, 104–108
Mansfield House, 45
Market analysis, 37, 39
    segmentation, 34, 35, 36, 37
    research, 38, 40, 48, 50, 163
Marketing, 22, 25, 27, 32, 34, 52, 80, 81,
    122, 142, 143–158, 163
    direct, 151, 152
Marketing plan, 144–146
Media, 149, 150, 152
Meeting, how to run, 101
Menu, costing, 73, 77, 79, 89, 109
    types, 82
    writing, 81, 82, 83, 84, 85, 109
Metropole, 31
Millbrook, 34
Minimum Wage Act 1983, 60
Monopoly, 43
Moore, Geoffrey, 25
Moore, Mike, 32

N

Negotiate, how to, 100
Newsletter, 146, 151
New Zealand School of Food and Wine,
    112, 155, 158
Non-customers, 158, 161
Non-English speakers, 132
Non-verbal communication, 130
Nouvelle cuisine, 13

O

Occupational safety, 142

P

Pacific Rim cuisine, 13
Pandoro, 32
Parental Leave and Employment Act
    1987, 60
Parken, Michael, 42
Pedro, 31, 144
Pegasus Bay Winery, 146
Perfect competition, 45
Personal guarantees, 28, 56, 57

Personal renewal, 160
Personal space, 131
Peters, Tom, 18, 43, 81, 93
Pizza Hut, 41, 72
Porter, Michael, 41
Power, 41, 48, 79, 96
    leadership, 94
Press release, writing a, 146, 149, 150
Price, 29, 36, 39, 43, 44, 45, 60, 70, 144
    price-led costing, 74
    what's in a price, 70
Price elasticity, 70
Pricing strategies, 72
Privacy Act 1993, 59, 117, 151
Psychographics, 33, 36

Q

Quality, 30, 43, 147
    check, 127, 128
    experience, 18
    perception, 19, 70
    TQM, 124–128

R

Relationships, 122, 123, 125, 130, 146
Relationship marketing, 145
Renewal, 159–164
Resource Management Act 1991, 58
Restaurant, 9, 10, 12, 13, 16, 17, 20, 25, 31,
    32, 33, 35, 38, 41, 42, 54, 57, 63, 64, 65,
    66, 72, 81, 82, 83, 161, 162, 163
    BYO, 88
    costing, 73, 77
    experience, 20
    maitre d'hôtel, 105
    merchandise, 157
    relationships, 122
    security, 106
    set-up costs, 66
    upselling, 157
    wine list, 86
Restaurant Brands, 41
Restaurant manager, responsibilities,
    104–108
Restaurant reviews, 24, 25, 124, 146
Roddick, Anita, 23, 28, 152, 166
Rules of good service, 129

S

Safe food, rules, 134–142
Safety in the kitchen, 142
Saggio di Vino, 43
Sale of Goods Act 1908, 57
Sale of Liquor Act 1989, 9, 10
Sales, forecasting, 64
Scarcity, 42
Scholz, Lisa, 43
Schuster, Daniel, 146
Scott, Allan, 33
Seagar, Jo, 32
Shutdown, 46
Signature dishes, 31
Starbucks, 31, 41, 147
Stephanie's, 162
Stock takes, 62, 77, 106
Strategic alliances, 146
Strategy, 21, 23, 30, 31, 101, 102
    business, 161, 162
    pricing, 69, 70
    skimming, 72
Strawberry Fare, 31
Stronechrubie, 33
Success, foundations of, 164
Summary dismissal, 120
Supply, law of, 43, 44
S.W.O.T., 38, 160
Synergy, 33

T

Talk the talk, 144
Team, building a, 27, 93–102
Technology adoption cycle, 25, 26
The George Hotel, 33
The Strip, 42, 45
Thornley, Peter, 85, 124
Time-temperature abuse, 138–142
TQM, 124, 125, 126
    Deming Chain, 127

V

Viaduct Basin, 42, 45
Vinnies, 163
Vision, 21, 23, 27, 29, 30, 31, 53, 81, 93, 94,
    95, 97, 102, 143, 148, 163

W

Wages Protection Act 1983, 60
Waters, Alice, 15
Why businesses fail, 163
Wilderness Lodge, 33
Wine list, writing, 86, 87
    matching with food, 89–92
    opening, 92, 127, 128